Picking Wings
Off
Butterflies

PICKING WINGS OFF BUTTERFLIES

A Father and Son TBI Memoir

Scott R. Stahlecker
With Excerpts by David S. Stahlecker

PICKING WINGS OFF BUTTERFLIES
A FATHER AND SON TBI MEMOIR

Copyright © 2017 Scott R. Stahlecker.

All rights reserved. No part of this book may be used or reproduced by any means, graphic, electronic, or mechanical, including photocopying, recording, taping or by any information storage retrieval system without the written permission of the author except in the case of brief quotations embodied in critical articles and reviews.

iUniverse books may be ordered through booksellers or by contacting:

iUniverse
1663 Liberty Drive
Bloomington, IN 47403
www.iuniverse.com
1-800-Authors (1-800-288-4677)

Because of the dynamic nature of the Internet, any web addresses or links contained in this book may have changed since publication and may no longer be valid. The views expressed in this work are solely those of the author and do not necessarily reflect the views of the publisher, and the publisher hereby disclaims any responsibility for them.

Any people depicted in stock imagery provided by Thinkstock are models, and such images are being used for illustrative purposes only. Certain stock imagery © Thinkstock.

ISBN: 978-1-5320-2621-8 (sc)
ISBN: 978-1-5320-2620-1 (e)

Library of Congress Control Number: 2017910688

Print information available on the last page.

iUniverse rev. date: 07/18/2017

This book is dedicated to cultivating compassion and raising awareness of the challenges facing the less fortunate. It is my hope that it will inspire others to engage in actions that will foster positive social change.

David Stahlecker

CONTENTS

Preface xi
Chapter 1   David Doesn't Mind If You Stare 1
Chapter 2   Laughter, Nature's Best Medicine 10
Chapter 3   "The Car That Hit Me Sent Me Flying" 22
Chapter 4   The Boy Who Wouldn't Wake Up 32
Chapter 5   When Hope Fails 43
Chapter 6   Above and Beyond the Call of Duty 52
Chapter 7   Sauerkraut Never Tasted So Good 58
Chapter 8   One Step at a Time 66
Chapter 9   Led Astray in Handcuffs 77
Chapter 10 A Sex Change 83
Chapter 11 Fires on the Home Front 95
Chapter 12 "Disabled People Think Different" 107
Chapter 13 Separation Anxiety 116
Chapter 14 Lowering Expectations 124
Chapter 15 Surviving Adolescence 136
Chapter 16 "North to the Future!" 147
Chapter 17 Guilt by Association 157
Chapter 18 Our National Shame 166
Chapter 19 Letters from Jail 178
Afterword 193

PREFACE

The story you are about to read is a true story—reasonably true anyway, because no bard on earth has a perfect memory. Suffice it to say, the exotic locales in which this book takes place—from Hawaii, to the European continent, to the Wild West, to Asia, and northward to Alaska—are accurate. Regarding the conversations and descriptions of what took place at these destinations, most were gleaned from journals and memories, or they describe real-time events I happened to be experiencing while writing the first draft. Can I swear that what you are about to read is 100 percent truthful? In spirit, yes. In a court of law, perhaps not. And as most disclaimers go, I must state that only a few of the names contained in this account needed to be changed.

This is a father-and-son odyssey about life, which centers on an overachieving father—played by myself—and my beloved son, who suffered a traumatic brain injury (TBI) at age six. My overall objective in writing this story was to share a candid portrayal of what it's like raising a child with a TBI and to offer a source of inspiration for other parents, caregivers and healthcare professionals. In addition, my hope is that the experiences David endured within these pages will also serve as a rallying cry for better treatment of the physical and emotionally challenged individuals within our society and the criminal justice system.

Many books involving human tragedy often spin the narration in an effort to prove that unfortunate events can be chalked up to fate or a divine will. Consequently, much of the literature involving real-life dramas asks readers to consider that there is a purpose for human suffering. My goal, however, was to write a more truthful piece, one that reflects what most people actually experience. This is not a fairy tale in which all things work out for the better; rather, it's a piece that emphasizes the blatantly obvious: tragedy sucks. Because for many individuals who endure the gravest of misfortunes, life will never get better. So as the author, I feel there's only one way to tell David's story that will have merit. It's to convey to readers how they will—when confronted with real tragedy—experience a barrage of emotions and questionable thoughts that they never fathomed they were capable of experiencing. Confronting one's deep inner self is really the catharsis that enables us to better understand and accept what life throws our way; it permits us to find real answers, rather than to be pacified by false hope.

Despite the drama contained within these pages, this story is really meant to be an enjoyable, hilarious, and enlightening tale. David wouldn't have it any other way. And when you get to know David through his crazy escapades, you'll realize for yourself how important it is *not* to take life so seriously. For in spite of David's injuries, he's an extremely gregarious fellow, a socialite extraordinaire, and his carefree attitude is contagious. If people can be enriched and entertained by his struggles, then by all means, a little humor on his behalf is fine by him. After all, laughter is nature's best medicine, or so goes chapter 2.

Picking Wings Off Butterflies

Although I penned the following pages, I can't really take credit for the story. For this is the story of David's life, a journey I am honored to share and one I felt duty-bound to truthfully express. If you find the many anecdotes that follow are entertaining and beneficial, it's because David experienced and survived these events. If I can take any credit, it's only because I'm his father (as well as a writer), who simply wanted to do a good job at honoring the life of my son.

Lastly, I want to mention that David also contributed greatly to the contents of this book. While writing the first draft, I often asked him to write down his own thoughts in a journal so that I could accurately portray his feelings, ideas, and memories. The italicized excerpts of this book reflect those thoughts from his journal, which I've included with little or no grammatical changes to retain the authenticity of his voice. I also consulted with him every step of the way, because I wanted him to be comfortable with the parts of his life we mutually chose to reveal. Ultimately, he was the one wielding the editorial ax as we worked together in the telling of this journey.

Scott Stahlecker

CHAPTER 1

DAVID DOESN'T MIND IF YOU STARE

ST. GEORGE, UTAH, 2006

*D*avid doesn't want your pity, but he doesn't mind if you stare. There he sits, the left side of his face drooping slightly, the corner of his mouth suspended in a delicate, permanent frown. Today he's sporting mix-match threads, an oversized T-shirt, a pair of filthy tennis shoes he borrowed from a friend, and camouflage pants shredded at the hems.

His arms are speckled with tattoos. Some homemade, some professional, some professionally painted to cover up the worst of the homemade ones. The tats are chaotic, prompted by the compulsivity to express his inner rebel. There's the burning cross, a gigantic medieval dragon, two dangling skull cherries, a Celtic rose, and a Celtic dragon. There's a large tat done in bold letters above his left elbow that shouts the name of his hero OZZY!

Seven, homemade ink letters pepper the fingers on his left hand spelling his nickname, Skooter. David has always had a hard time planning ahead. So when he ran out of fingers and had more letters, he simply dropped down a knuckle and worked his way back across his hand.

He acquired another tat this year. This one consists of the ten letters of his last name leaping three inches high in Old English lettering spanning his shoulder blades. How did he pay for this tattoo? He traded his black, shiny moped to a friend—the would-be tattoo artist—for a deal that amounts to roughly one hundred bucks a letter.

I told him, "Look at the bright side, David. When you're sitting at home because you don't have any wheels, you can at least look at your back in a mirror and know who you are!"

Depending on the week, David will be sporting a different haircut. This week his noggin is showing a week and a half of growth after having been sheared like a lamb down to the bristles. A month from now it will resemble a decent barbershop cut and cap him with an air of intelligence. David will then shave the sides of his head to slash out a jagged Mohawk. As the weeks progress, the lines of the Mohawk will become more irregular, because not even a normal person can hold a razor in one hand, a handheld mirror in his other hand, and then bounce his reflection off the bathroom mirror and expect to cut straight lines.

What follows will be three weeks of spiked hair in which he looks like a pineapple. His mother, Gena, and I joke with him about his unflattering hairstyles, because advice sinks in better for him after a good laugh. About the time we convince him the Mohawk must go, he promptly shaves most of it off, starting from the crown of his head and working his way forward. But he always leaves the bangs, split by a cowlick, which dangle over his forehead for a few more weeks like a pasted-on mustache until he shaves his head again and repeats the entire process. I know this will happen again and again, because he's been repeating this obsessive cycle since his near-death experience over two decades ago.

David requires an enormous amount of time and energy, which will become evident in the telling of his story. After decades of caring for David, I'm sad to report my cache of patience is about exhausted. I've become much harder on the lad as the years have progressed. However, if I'm free to give myself the benefit of the doubt, maybe I became the way I am out of necessity. For when it comes to the sheer number and magnitude of the unfortunate circumstances that transpire in David's life, I've learned how to decipher the real emergencies from the imaginary ones.

Just the other day, Gena and I were vacationing in Idaho where we were eager to spend a few days relaxing around a campfire by the Snake River without getting any calls from David. Why we were stupid enough to be so optimistic I don't know, because we'd never left David alone for more than a few days without a manufactured catastrophe occurring.

Dana, my daughter, called the day after we arrived in Idaho and said, "David's driven himself to the emergency room on his moped. He thinks he's having another heart attack."

This was David's third heart attack of the month. Should we have been worried? As parents, we're obligated to be worried, but are we duty-bound to experience the pandemonium of thinking our child is having a heart attack for what must be the twentieth time in a year?

He's in good hands, we convinced ourselves. *He's at the hospital, and we're a day away anyway. Thank goodness he has Medicaid.* A few hours later, we got the expected call from Dana that he was okay. We drove back to St. George the following Monday. I told Gena (her being the greatest of all mothers and me playing the unsympathetic dad) that one of these days David's going to fall asleep on his arm and it will go numb and then he'll really think he's having a heart attack! (David's gotten into the habit of reading one of Gena's old nursing diagnostic textbooks, which advised him that tingling in the arm may represent the onset of a heart attack.) Guess what happened on Tuesday? David woke up, called us from his apartment, and convinced Gena he was having yet another heart attack. Away to the emergency room they flew. I stayed home and mowed the lawn. Needless to say, the signs and symptoms miraculously disappeared by the time he was checked in to the hospital. Hours passed. (It was the emergency room.) David wanted to go home. He said, "I don't have time for this kind of son-of-a-bitchin-fuckin-bullshit." (His penchant for cussing will soon be revealed.) Gena forced him to wait and see the doctor, hoping the experience might deter him from crying wolf the next day.

A doctor finally had time for David and asked, "What were you doing when you noticed your arm was tingling?"

"I was sleeping, and when I woke up, my arm hurt."

And then the doctor gave him $500.00 worth of emergency room medical advice. "That can happen when you're sleeping, David. Your arm might fall asleep, but it doesn't mean you're having a heart attack."

A few days later, he got word that the brother of his girlfriend was going to kick his butt. Bullies have been using David as a punching bag to satisfy their sadistic proclivities ever since they realized how vulnerable David can be. I wanted to tell the brute, "Why don't you pick on someone who doesn't have a brain injury?" but I let it drop. At David's age, my involvement only weakens his stature among his friends. But David was hysterical, and his mind was conjuring up all kinds of ways he'd bleed. He would not go back to his apartment to sleep, or shower, or change, or eat, or brush his teeth.

When he received the call and first learned of the bully's intentions, he rode his moped over to his grandma's apartment wearing my old army jacket I'd given him and his pajama bottoms. During the next four days, he hid out in her living room and slept on her couch, no doubt parting the curtains every time he heard the neighbors passing by. Not until day five did he manage to gather enough guts to sleep in his own bed. Monetary incentive might have boosted his courage. We told him that he would not get his allowance until he went back to his apartment.

Now, for reasons that profoundly disturbed me, the police in St. George had him pegged as a druggie or a drunk. Officers would stop him for merely stumbling down the sidewalk. I'd log the random checks down on paper, anticipating that I'd need to present documentation of the infractions to a lawyer one day. My log grew to four pages in length, even though I skipped writing all the superfluous details. On average, the police "interviewed" him once a month over a three-year period. The interviews were part of a new policing trend in which the force was trying to better know the members of the community (I was matter-of-factly informed one day). Funny, the officers never took the time to introduce themselves to me, probably because I didn't stumble along the sidewalk with a bad limp. Or maybe they were just getting to know certain kinds of people whom they planned to one day be ferrying over to the jailhouse.

I really can't blame the police, can I? David is on prescription drugs and walks like a drunk. Who wouldn't, if one leg was shorter than the other, having been snapped at the thigh and pinned with steel bolts? David walks on his tiptoes to compensate for one leg being shorter than the other. His equilibrium will never recover since his head bounced off the hood of that car, hurling him down the street into another parked car where he collapsed lifeless in the middle of the road.

David possesses a prehistoric concept of the value of money. Ten dollars is a hundred dollars is a thousand dollars. What he knows is that money is the most sought-after commodity and spoils like milk if he doesn't spend it all in one day. Give him any amount of cash, and as long as there's a store or restaurant open, he won't stop buying or eating until his pockets are empty. On a good day—on an exceptionally rare day—he'll keep a few bucks to buy cigarettes for the following day.

We've tried everything to teach him to be responsible with his allowance. If we give him all his cash at the beginning of the month, we'll be paying his way through the next twenty-nine days. Give him money twice a month and it only spares us a day or two of him begging for more. Once a week works okay, but a few bucks every day works best. The trouble is, it's not fun or convenient handing out a tiny allowance to a grown man every morning, especially since he lives across town.

We used to buy David electronics—televisions, stereos, game consoles, CDs, DVDs, and the like. Each year at Christmas and on his birthday, we vow never to buy him electronics again. We've yet to keep this vow. What David has hawked at pawnshops could pay for his college education—if he could focus long enough to earn a degree. After three failed attempts at college, I'm convinced a higher education is not in his deck of cards.

The nice individuals at the vocational rehabilitation center in Utah tried their best to move David forward in life, but David let them down too many times for them to take him seriously again. Their latest attempt to better David was to set him up in an electronics apprenticeship. I thought about giving David a reality check and telling him how difficult this program would be, but I couldn't find it in my heart to dash his hopes. The program takes years to complete and requires oodles of mathematical skills. I wondered why the guidance counselor thought he could tackle the program in the first place. As I'd guessed, David lost interest in the program a week later, which spared him from experiencing yet another failed attempt at life.

David knows tomorrow will come, but planning for this obvious inevitability is slightly beyond his mental prowess. One thinks he would mourn the dawn and dread the approaching dusk as the sun creeps around the world bringing yet another day of challenges, yet this isn't the case. David's thrilled to be alive, and he's so excited for every fresh new start that it's almost impossible for him to get a good night's sleep. His sleeping habits are more like that of a typical house cat. In general, a twenty-four-hour period for him is divided among moments of alertness, occasional napping and spacing out throughout the day, and then staying up to the wee hours of the night.

Dealing with David's disability income, subsidized housing benefits, and food stamps is a horrendous nightmare. All three benefits are run by different governmental agencies requiring fantastical amounts of paperwork. Even a minute fluctuation in David's income by way of a job—or possibly the cash found in his birthday cards—could cause his benefits to decrease or be eliminated altogether. Most recently, he got a seasonal job that lasted just a few months, and this caused a substantial drop in his disability income. After the job ended, his compensation was so screwed up that he suffered a significant loss of income. Gena spent a full year and countless hours trying to recoup his losses but finally gave up. Lesson learned. It is far less stressful for Gena and me to encourage David not to be a productive member of society and, consequently, far less productive for society not to have wonderful people like David contributing to it.

When the government has questions or needs facts, there are threats made to cut benefits for not getting an agency a few bits of information within a specific deadline. Normally, these requests come by way of a form letter, dated late in the process, and delivered just days before the response is due. Pity the person who needs questions answered to meet these deadlines. Just try calling one of these help lines and listening to a recording with seven different options, which fails to mention option eight—the option you need!

If and when you do get through to a real voice on the phone, expect a two-month delay from the date you thought the problem would be solved. Next, plan to take a day off when you realize nothing was solved and you have to start all over. Take names, write detailed notes, document, and then push, push, push for the rights of your child, because few will.

And it's not like David's trying to bleed the welfare system dry. David likes to work and wants to work, but his injuries prevent him from consistently working. He can't do long hours by the day, and he can't maintain the focus required of him to hold a job for more than a few weeks. His pattern has been to start a full-time job and in a week or so he's usually down to part time, because he can't handle the workload. Often, this process is not entirely his fault. In the real world most bosses lack the patience or experience to deal with a person who has suffered a brain injury.

No, David doesn't want your pity, despite the fact that

Picking Wings Off Butterflies

I've offered a smattering of reasons as to why you should take pity on him. Here I have erred and beg your pardon. David is my son—my firstborn and only son. If you are a parent, perhaps you can understand my disappointment that David was robbed of a normal life at such a tender age.

CHAPTER 2

LAUGHTER, NATURE'S BEST MEDICINE

KENAI, ALASKA, 2007

There's more to David's life than my cynical ranting has led you to believe. My only excuse for meandering through my melancholy state of mind is because it's so easy to focus on the negatives. Finding the riches to David's life is like panning for gold. The nuggets of his goodness are always lying right there below the surface. I just have to sift through the rubble to get to them. Lest you think me hopelessly insensitive, let me share with you a few of the reasons why David means so much to me.

Although David doesn't understand the concept of money, if you need a buck, he's willing to give you all the money he has wadded up in his pockets. Friends particularly like this quality in him. They'll stick to him like leeches on blood sausage when he's got a fistful of cash. Need beer,

Picking Wings Off Butterflies

chips, and junk food for an impromptu party? He's buying. Are you almost out of gas? No problem. He'll spot you the money to top off your tank.

David also has a voracious appetite. The one thing he's always hungry for? Chinese buffet. He'd pay for my lunch every day for eternity if he had the funds. It's rare that I let him pay for lunch, but I do so on occasion, because giving does the heart good and David gets a kick out of treating dear old Dad. I usually throw in the tip, because David can't compute the 15 percent extra. After getting our fill of sushi and orange chicken, he's stumped when the cashier asks him for more money, since the concept of tax eludes him as well.

Recently, when David heard I'd lost my job as the manager of a local trucking company, we were driving to a barbecue out toward Kenai, Alaska. David yelled to me from the backseat of Gena's Subaru, "Dad, they need help raking leaves at the apartment where I'm working. You *wanna* job?"

I considered the prospect of working for chump change doing kids' work, which was my very first job I did for a neighbor when I was seven years old living in Makakilo, Hawaii. "No. But thanks anyways, Dave."

David aims to please, and his generosity is authentic. He's the most generous person I know, and not just with money. Being the middle-aged man I am, now in my late forties, there are times when I need an extra hand. David will work for me all day for gas or cigarette money. It's not that I'm cheap. When times are good, I've paid him by the hour. Then there are those times when I just need his free help around the house, because he's my son and because I don't want to treat him like an employee. David is usually happy to oblige and rarely complains.

These days, working around the house usually involves clearing dead spruce pine trees killed by the appropriately named spruce beetle. This pesky insect crawled its way across Alaska via Canada all the way down to the Homer Spit, which is pretty much the farthest one *can* spit in northwest America. Homer's an eclectic little village best known by locals as "a quaint drinking village with a fishing problem." Many trees on my property have already toppled over since they've been drilled full of holes by the aforementioned beetle. The remaining standing dead trees need to be axed Paul Bunyan–style. I don't swing an ax, so it's a joy felling the beasts the modern way with my eighteen-inch chainsaw. Once they've magnificently crashed to the ground, I limb the branches off and chainsaw the trunk into sections, which I later split into firewood with a mechanized splitter. I cannot, under any circumstances, let David use the chainsaw. This would be too irresponsible. This entire grueling process takes a lot of brute strength. I employ David for help, along with my trusty all-terrain vehicle with a trailer, so that we can haul our firewood back up to the house.

Working with David is like working with a new recruit in training. I tell him what to do and where to go, and then verify that he understands the task. He needs constant direction and has a hard time anticipating what needs to be done next. If I tell him what to do and how to do it, he'll keep on doing it until his energy putters out. Coffee, cigarettes, and food extend his productivity, but like the effects of a sugary energy drink, David eventually crashes. He's half my age, but I run circles around him. What matters, however, is that he is *so* willing to help *all* the time.

David has the uncanny aptitude to remember numbers. He can recall obvious numbers such as his license number and Social Security number, but he can also remember the addresses and street names of places we've lived. He's great with phone numbers too. For while he may not be that adept at utilizing all of the functions of a modern phone, he more than makes up for this by being able to remember the phone numbers to all of his friends.

His spelling abilities are also off the charts. Big, long, complicated words are as easy for him to spell as simple words. He's the family dictionary when we play Scrabble. I can almost see his mind turning as he spells words out. Maybe his brain was jarred into having a more advanced phonetic system, one in which his mental capacities can visualize precisely where the vowels and consonants of a word automatically go.

David's also good with names, particularly the names of actors and musicians. You know how difficult it is to remember the name of a movie or the actor in a movie? Give David a brief description of the movie, and he'll likely tell you the name of the movie and who starred in it. Every once in a while, however, he'll look at an actor on screen and draw a complete blank. If I know who the actor is, I'll tell him, and at this point he's able to rattle off other movies the actor was in. It's like he's fishing for memories by picturing words instead of relying on visual cues.

His shortcomings in visual recognition are more notable for places we've been to, and he also possesses an odd inability to match different types of scenery with familiar locales. Through the years, we've moved and traveled often. (Both my children lived or traveled through dozens of states and half a dozen countries before they were ten.) I remember one particular trip as we were traveling to Houston from Austin, Texas. David looked out the window and thought we were in Missouri. He'd been to Missouri before, but apparently the foliage he was watching pass by tricked him into forgetting what state we were in.

Not only does David have difficulty matching where

he's been to where he's going based on the unique scenery, but he also lacks the ability to estimate the time it takes to get from one place to another. I can tell David it will take two hours to get from Austin to Houston, but an hour and a half into the trip, he'll think we still have three hours to go. In other words, he's long forgotten the amount of time I initially told him it would take, and he's failed to recognize the amount of time we've been on the road. A three-hour trip must seem like a lifetime for him to travel, which is probably why every time we hit the road he tries to sleep the entire trip. I wonder why David isn't interested in the excitement of traveling. Heck, just getting in the car and hitting the road is adventure enough for me. And what of the thrill of taking longer trips into distant lands and cultures? David cares little of these experiences.

A few years back, we took a family trip down to Mexico, south of Cancun. For a week we swam in the waves of pristine beaches, shopped for a day on the island of Cozumel, took a white-knuckle flight (in which we got lost in the clouds) to see the ancient Mayan ruins of Tulum and Chichen Itza, snorkeled in lagoons filled with exotic sea creatures at the Xel-Ha Aquatic Adventure Park, and enjoyed golfing and scuba diving. Who was absent on all of these family excursions? David. We'd paid for an all-inclusive package at the resort. As long as we were wearing the resort's bracelet, we could eat and drink to our heartburn's content. David thought he'd died and gone to heaven. He ate and drank himself silly through the warm Mexican nights and by day slept off his hangovers.

To his credit, David loves people. He loves meeting and greeting and being with people. He's a socialite extraordinaire. On the trip to Mexico, the reason he didn't want to visit any exotic places was because he wanted to be

Picking Wings Off Butterflies

with exotic people. Ancient ruins, snorkeling, chasing manta rays and sea turtles, window-shopping, getting sunburned—these were things David didn't want to experience. His idea of fun was meeting new people. The fact that the drinking age in Mexico is eighteen also slightly curbed his desire to explore. And given that there was an Ozzy look-alike from the Netherlands also vacationing at the hotel was too much for David to resist. So he and the Ozzy character stayed poolside by the bar.

You'd love hearing David howl with laughter. His laugh goes unchecked by any inhibitions. This is no doubt due to one of the injuries he sustained to his brain in the area known as the frontal lobe region. The frontal lobe is pretty much the desktop of the brain. Take a hit to this area and every personality trait a person has can get scrambled. This certainly explains a lot in David's case. David's laugh is so wholehearted it can make him pee his pants. If you didn't think the joke was funny, just watching David laugh will make you laugh. He's infectious.

As for me, I've forgotten how to laugh. I smile and make noises that mimic laughing, but I don't really laugh. When I succeed at snorting, it surprises me, as though an imposter has hijacked my throat. I don't laugh enthusiastically due to all the crap that has happened in David's life and, to some degree, the sensitivity I've acquired in response to all the crap that happens on this spinning planet. For many years, I even thought I'd lost the right to laugh . . .

I wish I could laugh as he laughs. I envy him. Him laughing without a care in the world, because in many respects, his injuries prevent him from having a care in the world, and me, bearing the brunt of his load through life, acting silent as a deaf mute. It's a crying shame.

A few days ago, David was standing in my kitchen eating

Fig Newtons after dipping them in milk. As I walked into the kitchen, he eyed a fig cookie suspiciously and asked me, "What kind of fruit is in these cookies?"

Knowing David, I knew he wasn't joking and needed this mystery solved. I began slowly so that my choice of words would hopefully sink in. "Are you sure there is nothing, nothing whatsoever on the packaging, that tells you what is in THE *Fig* Newtons?"

He studied the wrapper long and hard. "Nothing."

"What about figs, David?"

Yesterday, I was standing on the balcony outside Dana and Stix's apartment. (And by the way, when I say "a few days ago" or "yesterday" etc., I really do mean yesterday and a few days ago at the time of writing.) David comes out of his apartment (he happens to live just two doors down) and yells at me to come take a look at his water purifier. David's referring to the water filter pitcher Gena bought him to help filter out the toxins from the tap. In some areas of Alaska, the water is an unquenchable shade of orange on account of the heavy iron content. David walks toward me, saying, "The pitcher's been broken for a week, and I can't fix it."

While we walk to his apartment, I take a moment to mentally troubleshoot the possible ways that would prevent the pitcher from operating correctly. There's the clear plastic pitcher, a round white insert that fits into the top of the pitcher, and a filter that slides into the white insert. Seems simple enough. We get to his kitchen, and I check it out. It takes me a fraction of a second to figure out the problem. There's a thin piece of plastic on the side of the filter that is supposed to slip into a groove in the white insert. I slide the filter into its groove and fill the insert with water. David stares at the water droplets that are now miraculously trickling into the clear pitcher. His expression tells me he thinks I've performed the most amazing of magical feats.

"How? Oh my God! That's so stupid!" He laughs uncontrollably and heads for the bathroom.

When he returns, I tell him, "You know what I'm going to get you for your birthday? One of those toys with differently shaped blocks that you slip into specific holes in a ball. You know, the red square goes into the square hole, the yellow triangle goes into the triangularly shaped hole, and the blue round ball goes into the round hole. That could help you solve these kinds of riddles."

Sometimes David does things that make me wag my head. Other times, he does things that make me want to cry.

Because that very next Monday after fixing David's water pitcher, I heard Gena's cell phone ringing in her purse and I flipped the receiver open. It was a guy from Texas I'd never talked to before. His raspy, singsong voice had a peculiar feminine quality to it, and he sounded furious. He said he was looking for David's mother. Being the good husband that I am and wanting to spare Gena the grief of dealing with the angry man, I lied and stated, "She's not here. I'm David's father. What's this about?"

"I want you to speak to David and ask him to stop coming on to my husband."

Surely the guy meant to say he wanted David to stop messing with his wife. "I don't understand," I said.

"I want you to tell David that Freddy is my husband and to stop flirting with him."

Ahh, I did hear you right the first time, I thought. But the conversation still made no sense. David was in Alaska. This guy was in Texas. Some guy thought David had been flirting with . . . his husband? *How's this possible, and how long has my son been gay?* I wondered.

"I'll talk to David," I assured the man.

I got off the phone and slowly said to David, "That was the most bizarre phone call I have ever received in my entire life. Are you gay now?"

"Yes," he replied out of spite.

Not that it matters to me if someone's a homosexual (and that's the honest-to-God-strike-me-down-dead truth). But David's not gay. How do I know this? Because these days the inquiring minds of parents want to know if their children are gay, so we watch for the approaching signs of sexual maturity our kids exhibit when they come of age. That's how. And David clearly was interested in the opposite sex. The really sad part of this story is not that David flirted with a guy on the phone. As strange as this scenario sounds, what's sad is this is just the kind of event that happens in David's life, which is totally within the realm of possibilities on any given day. And the real tragedy is that David really doesn't know who or what he is, but he'll experiment to find the answer.

He's a victim waiting to be victimized.

The following week I was visiting David back at his apartment in Kenai and glanced at the paint-by-numbers kit I had bought him. The scene he was painting was of a majestic bald eagle soaring over autumn-tinted trees with a backdrop of snow-capped mountain peaks not unlike the picturesque views we saw every day living in the land of the midnight sun. David was halfway through completing the painting.

"This is looking pretty good," I told him, because it was genuinely impressive.

I took a gander at the instructions on the table next to the painting. There was an 11" x 14" replica of the painting on paper. Similar to the painting, the replica was divided into hundreds of puzzle-like portions with microscopic letters and numbers printed inside each portion. Next to the replica was the instruction sheet, which described in complex numerical and alphabetical codes how to mix particular colors by using only the primary and secondary colors supplied with the paint kit.

"I'd shoot myself if I had to do this painting," I joked to him.

I had bought the paint kit because he liked to draw in pencil, and I'd been trying his entire life to interest him in using color. He surprised me by rising to the challenge. The painting would've required far too much patience for me to tackle. I was left wondering how David had the ability to break the complex numerical and alphabetical coloring code and then spend hours painting with microscopic detail, yet he had tried unsuccessfully for a week to get his water pitcher to work by simply lining up two pieces of plastic.

That's David in a nutshell. It's impossible to tell what he can do from what he can't do, and what he wants to do from what he's unmotivated to do.

On another wall in his "painting studio" was a huge drawing he'd been working on for months. This particular work was expanding with his imagination. He'd been Scotch-taping additional 8.5" x 11" sheets of white paper together to enlarge the masterpiece. It was not uncommon for him to fill his walls in this manner with many drawings. When he was younger, and we lived in San Antonio, Texas, he didn't use paper at all, instead sketching directly onto his walls. I had given him permission to do this, of course. Frankly, I thought it easier to paint his walls when we moved out of the house rather than do battle with him every day.

I studied the themes in this drawing, which were reminiscent of his tattoos. There was a castle with a dragon in the sky and stairs leading up from the castle toward the sky into an imaginary world. Off to the side of the castle were medieval, human-like creatures in skeletal form. (Bones are among David's many fascinations.) The detail in the drawing was impeccable, but the proportions were warped as though one chugged down a beer and was looking at the drawing through the bottom of the bottle.

I'd long since given up trying to impress David with the necessity of getting the proportions right. "People will appreciate your art more if they can recognize what you are actually trying to draw, David. Stay in the lines!" I'd told him at least a hundred times.

His inability to understand why it was so important to follow this advice has backfired on me, because there are many lessons in life that David has actually taught me. Two lessons come to mind at this juncture. First, David helped me discard the pretentious assumption that living life is all about staying in the lines. Living within the confines of someone else's outline for your life is a bad idea—and boring. Life is not a paint-by-numbers kit. Rules and traditions should be challenged with each successive generation. And when it comes to being a painter, writer, or musician or engaging in any kind of artistic adventure, one should follow one's own heart, because with today's commercialized mentality, originality is a human trait on the verge of extinction.

The second lesson is related to the first lesson. It can only be properly experienced by those who have not sidestepped tragedy and have otherwise dealt with human suffering for months, years, and even decades. The lesson is that life is not perfect; it's not meant to be experienced as though everyone were running on a treadmill in a linear path toward a similar goal. No matter where we live in this world, our particular cultures present an idyllic path to happiness and success.

Taking this path works reasonably well for "normal" people. It works especially well for families with the financial resources and connections to pave a path to success for their children. Not so, however, for those among us who are not normal.

So draw like you want to, David. Live like you want to.

CHAPTER 3

"THE CAR THAT HIT ME SENT ME FLYING"

FLASHBACK TO 1989

I remember that day clearer than I was probably intended to remember it. It was a school day and I was six years old and walking home from school with a friend of mine. We had to cross a street to get to the apartment housing complex, so I went first and was successful halfway across the street. And then it hit me. The car that hit me sent me flying.

Gena and I awoke that morning to a gentle tap on the door of an unfamiliar bedroom. I rolled to the edge of the bed, wondering where the light switch was. It took a few moments for my mind to register that I was not in Frankfurt, Germany, where I was serving in the army. I was in my father's home thousands of miles away in the seaside town of Oak Harbor, Washington.

22

Picking Wings Off Butterflies

I was dying to sleep in. I'd dreamt of sleeping in. For the past several years, I'd been forced to wake up at zero dark thirty and drive west out of Frankfurt to the suburb of Höchst in order to stand in the morning formation outside my company headquarters. Besides, Gena and I were on vacation. We were even on vacation from our children, who remained with my mother back in Frankfurt. After flying into Seattle the night before and driving to Oak Harbor, I was looking forward to spending a relaxing week with my father and stepmother.

I heard my father's house slippers pacing in the hallway just outside our door and remembered why I had asked him to wake us up. We had a long-awaited expedition ahead of us. A year earlier, I'd corresponded with a realtor in Montana and purchased twenty acres of mountain property in Helena. Gena and I intended to move to Montana after my tour in the army ended. Although we'd seen photos of the land and topographical maps, we needed to drive up and see the property to plot out the potential of the place. After a quick breakfast, we all jumped into my father's Mazda and traveled as far as Seattle before the sun even dawned. Other than the faint glow of the rising sun, there was nothing looming on the horizon, no impending sensation of doom in the forecast. By early afternoon, we'd driven as far as a rest stop outside Coeur d'Alene, Idaho. Fall had peaked. The aspens in the surrounding hills were blooming brilliant yellowish hues. The sting of approaching winter pricked my skin.

I would later conclude that David had stepped onto a busy street near our apartment in Frankfurt while walking home from school shortly before I awoke that morning. A few hours later, while he was fighting for his life, I was on a road trip bursting with excitement and thoughts of change.

Why it would be important for me to take a yellow

highlighter and strike a line between these two juxtaposed turn of events is one of those brain twists that I still cannot reconcile. The best analogy I can think of is the death of John Lennon. People can tell you exactly where they were the moment Lennon was shot in New York City. In a similar way, I place the time of David's accident in the early morning hours while I slept and his fight for survival during our trek east out of Washington State. But the analogy runs deeper than me just trying to remember what I was doing and how I was feeling when David was nearly killed. The memory stings, because someone—some supernatural agency—should have whispered in my ear and informed me that the beast of misfortune was standing right behind me getting ready to pounce.

At the moment when David was hit and thrown fifteen meters into another parked car, was I dreaming about the times my father drove me out to Dillingham Airfield on Oahu so I could learn how to fly sailplanes? When David bounced off the hood of the parked car and his head slammed against the pavement, was I smiling in my sleep shortly before dawn at one of the many jokes my father used to tell me? Was I gazing out the window when we whizzed through the panhandle of Idaho later that day, daydreaming of a log cabin in the woods, while physicians were drilling a hole in David's skull to relieve the mounting pressure building in his head that would inevitably lead to his brain damage?

Something magical or spiritual should be taking place when these kinds of events are transpiring in your life, when in fact nothing happens. *Nada. Nichts.* The reality is, parents can be thinking all kinds of frivolous thoughts at the precise moment their child is struck by a car, without a clue in the world it's happening and not a prayer of stopping it. This is a bizarre and cruel trick of life, especially if you're religious. Why? Because you have been praying hard all your life that such a thing would not happen. And, you have been walking diligently in the faith in exchange for the assurances of God that you and your family would be protected from this kind of thing from happening. Then it happens . . . and how you react to this fact-check can completely alter your religious outlook on life.

I don't recall feeling anything. It was a fast moment in my life, but when I look back it wasn't as fast as it seemed. Since the car accident I've become aware of the first person/ third person viewing. At the time it happened I remember seeing myself in the third person view like I was watching it happen. This doesn't sound realistic, but my only explanation for seeing it in the third person is maybe that I was aware of what was happening, although I can't recall anything.

I remember the walk home with my friend. I remember seeing my friend at one side of the street and me telling him to wait until I crossed the road. After getting halfway across the street, I remember being hit and at that point everything became like a blinking white light. It was like an old film where everything was filmed in black and white with the exception of the area between my neck and the top of my head. In this area I became aware of colors being dispersed like a loony-toon affect, but that's how it happened. At the time I felt like I was in a dream-like state, as though it was like something I was thinking about and not something that was actually happening. I'm told I almost died.

The sun was setting behind us as we drove east on Highway 12 through the last mountain pass at Forest Heights and down into the wide prairie where Helena is located. Low, watermelon-colored clouds stretched across the indigo sky as though pulled like cotton candy at both ends. I was disappointed by my first impression. Helena wasn't set in the mountains as I'd hoped. The city lies in the middle of a sunken valley with large, expansive slopes leading up into distant hills. Once we got out of the car to check in at the motel, I remember thinking the place looked colder than it felt.

We ate at a nearby diner. It felt good to stop rolling and have a decent meal. We'd traveled from Frankfurt, Germany, to Oak Harbor, Washington, the day before, and then from Oak Harbor to Helena, Montana. Since I was on vacation and my mind was still in a jet-lag fog, I'd given little thought about my mom, who was watching the kids, and the demands of my position as a tactical satellite systems operator. It was nice to see my dad again. Since moving with my mother in my early teens from the Hawaiian Islands to what the islanders call the mainland, I'd seen him only a half dozen times. Our last visit had been five years prior. I don't remember what we talked about while dining—likely just chitchat—but we were still having a great time catching up on missed memories.

Since my father and I rarely saw each other, I'd become accustomed to thinking of him as though he were a familiar stranger. I can still remember his soft-spoken voice, his handshake, and the warmth of a rare hug that we could only exchange between years of separation. We were not close, and may never have been close even if I'd lived with him after my parents divorced when I was nine. Still, there were things he'd do for me that reminded me that I was his son. Why he personally drove us out to Helena, I can't say. Being retired, maybe he was bored and had free time. Maybe he felt like taking a drive and getting out of town. But I'd

Picking Wings Off Butterflies

like to believe he wanted to spend time with Gena and me. Whatever his reason, I'm glad he was with me, because when we got back to the motel, my world changed forever.

The motel clerk notified me that I was to call the sheriff's office in Helena immediately. The sheriff informed me there had been an accident in Germany, and I was to call my army company. The noncommissioned officer on desk duty at Company C, Thirty-Second Signal Battalion, reported that my son had been hit by a car while walking home from school and gave me the number to the hospital. Through my broken German and the hospital staff's broken English, I was passed on to several German medical personnel and finally reached the physician who had been monitoring David in the hospital's critical care unit. David had suffered a massive head injury. He'd fractured his left femur. He was in a coma and was not expected to survive the next twenty-four hours.

Even now, the words I heard sound unbelievable. They are words that fall deafly, as though mouthed in a silent, black-and-white, slow-motion film sequence. These kinds of words are as implausible as they are unimaginable. No parent is prepared to hear such words, even less inclined to spend time worrying that such words would ever be uttered in reference to their child. Perhaps if I'd been in Frankfurt, maybe then could I have dared to believe what was happening. But I was halfway across the world, in a state I'd never traveled through, in a city I'd never visited, leaning against a pay phone with a sweaty black receiver dangling from my ear, hearing an obscene fable that only happens to other children and other parents. *Surreal* would not even begin to describe the world of confusion I found myself in.

How the army pulled it off I'll never know. But then again, in times of crisis, the armed forces are masters at logistics. When working as a team for a noble purpose, its personnel will sacrifice everything to render aid to those in conflict. Not surprisingly, then, at three o'clock in the morning, there was a knock on our motel door. I opened it to a member of the Red Cross. The elderly lady, donned in a white overcoat with a red cross stitched on the front pocket, handed me a one-way ticket to Frankfurt out of Great Falls, Montana, early that morning. She wished Gena and me well, was sorry she could not have done more, then departed mysteriously in the darkness of the early morning chill.

Just hours later I would be jarred out of my mental stupor and ushered back into reality at one of the airport's departing gates. Around me stood Gena, my father, and my stepmother, trying to comfort one another within our inconsolable circle of despair. I instinctively moved toward my father and began hugging him like I'd never hugged him before. I don't recall ever crying so profusely in my life. I've never cried that hard since. Somehow the good-byes got all rolled up into one. I knew it would be years before I'd see my father again, but when I hugged him, it was as though I was saying good-bye to my son—forever. And it was one of those body-convulsing, quaking, uncontrollable, and relentless cries of anguish that comes from deep down in the pit of your being, unleashing a grief you never thought humanly possible.

Gena was a watery blur when I stumbled over to her. She would not be traveling with me. We had left our passports and the rest of our baggage in Oak Harbor. As a member of the military, I could pass through customs with my military identification card. Gena would need her passport to get back to Germany. From the time we learned about David's accident, we were hedging our feelings. As a nurse, she'd seen a lot of pain and broken bodies through the years. I wondered

Picking Wings Off Butterflies

what she knew that she wasn't telling me. If she thought the worst, I couldn't tell. Her professional, curative attitude had engaged, and her words of encouragement were preventing me from thinking the worst. She resembled the pillar of motherhood—resilient and emotionally restrained—but I'm sure she was falling apart on the inside. We said our good-byes.

I was grateful to get a window seat on the plane. This way, I only had to engage a minimal number of flight attendants and passengers. By peering out the tiny window into the heavens, I became fixated on what became my shrunken universe of troubled thoughts and oppressive doubts. I'd been taught from early childhood that God dwells in the heavens somewhere above the blue. I could not have been physically closer to His presence than I was at that moment. If He was out there, He was evading my gaze. Since I couldn't see Him, I certainly expected to at least find Him in my thoughts. But there were no words of comfort or encouragement, no explanation for why He decided to allow this calamity to happen to my son.

When tragedy strikes someone you love, it invokes a radical shifting of one's spiritual perspective. It's as if your brain too were suddenly smacked and your hardened hypotheses were sent shattering into a kaleidoscope of prism-like reflections. What you have been taught about God is suddenly open for debate, and what you discover is that the excuses explaining why God allows suffering ring hollow.

Since the accident, people have told me, "God allowed this to happen to your son to teach you patience." Others have said, "God allowed this to happen to your son so that you and your family would learn to trust God." And not a few have implied, "God allows human suffering to continue because it is necessary to give people free will." And perhaps the most nonsensical, "God will not permit you or your son to suffer beyond what you can personally handle." Such proverbial clichés are found wanton of wisdom. For when you are in the moment, it's as if a line has been crossed. By virtue of being a participant in suffering, you earn the right to challenge these long-held assumptions about why God permits and condones human suffering. And not one explanation resonates as sensible, much less a soothing kernel of spiritual truth to ease the troubled soul.

Consider this: a good God would not allow these kinds of things to happen, because supreme compassion would empower Him to prevent and end all human suffering. I have settled this as a fact in my own mind. Because if I had the power to end human suffering, I would, and I certainly expect no less from a god. So if I could and would, and He cannot or will not, then His existence begins to tip in the direction of improbable. Given this twist of lucidity, the simple laws of cause and effect—at times so crude and at other times so fortuitous (yet so randomly metered out as to affect everyone impartially no matter what their position in life)—are natural laws that resonate as harmonious.

It would be years before my remonstrations to God would strike the final deathblow to my allegiance to religious dogma, and later, to bloom to fruition into a magnificent period of spiritual discovery. At the moment, however, I was absorbed with how much pain David was enduring and whether he was going to die. Even though I had the courage to ask the blasphemous questions, I was still trusting that God was in control, and I kept telling myself over and over again (as though by mere repetition my faith would be honored) that I could find a purpose for this accident lurking somewhere amid the moonlit luminescent clouds.

I also prayed for the worst! What else can a hopeless

parent, with nothing but the wishful notion of ending his child's suffering, do? For I asked God to take my son and be done with it. My motivation for bothering Him with such a mortal entreaty was clear: I didn't want my son to be a vegetable and live for decades hooked up to wires and tubes. I didn't want my son to be physically handicapped to the point that he couldn't enjoy life. I didn't want David to be mentally incompetent to the point where he was unable to think and act normally. All of these options would mean that David would be merely existing, which was far less than actually living. The last time I saw David, he was a healthy, vibrant young boy with a world of opportunity ahead of him.

Anything short of this perfection was unacceptable.

CHAPTER 4

THE BOY WHO WOULDN'T WAKE UP

I survived the accident and the next thing I can remember is waking up in an ambulance and seeing my grandma. Then I blacked out and there are several incidents where I remember something—then blackout. But that's how it was. I suppose that's because I kept coming out of my coma.

I don't recall how I got to the hospital after landing in Frankfurt, but I'll never forget standing before the seemingly impenetrable swinging doors leading to the intensive care unit of Universitätsklinikum. The doors to the university hospital's ICU had a yellowing, maple patina, and looked as if they would give a middle linebacker a challenge to push through. David had survived, this much I knew, yet the pain he might've been enduring petrified me. My imagination had also kept me sleepless on the long flight over as I considered all of the possible ways his injuries would affect his future. Assuming the possible scenarios had been futile. I needed to face David, confront what he was up against, and pushing through those doors was the only way to obtain my answers.

As the doors swung shut behind me with an echoing *thump, thump, thump,* I peered down the long, poorly lit corridor ahead. Indistinguishable noises and voices bounced out of several doors and across the shiny tile floor toward me. The stench of hospital assaulted my nostrils. I feared the suspense would be prolonged by having to make my way to each door and then peer into every room to find my son. Suddenly, a nurse popped out through one of the doors and walked my way. I told her who I was, then followed her tentatively as she led me through the first door on the right.

From a distance David looked like a miniature, white mummy. A soft blanket covered him from his toes all the way up across his chest. His head was bound by a maze of gauze. An oxygen mask, fogged with condensation, covered his mouth and nose. His head was enormous, like the head of a snowman, completely disproportionate to the rest of his tiny frame. For a moment I thought they'd wrapped his head with too much gauze, but as I got closer, it was apparent his head, eyelids, cheeks, and nose were severely swollen. The only recognizable feature that indicated to me that this was my son were his eyes—closed and bulging as they were—but the eyes were David's.

The nurse and I were soon joined by one of the physicians who had been treating David. His English was poor and offered with a thick German accent.

"David has bad head trauma," the doctor said. He pointed to the back of David's head where it rested against the pillow, but he didn't turn David's head so I could get a better view. "Right now, David is in a coma. When he arrived, he was unconscious. We keep him in the coma to help him heal."

I was skeptical. People spend years in comas and don't wake up. Putting a person into a coma didn't sound logical. This was the first time I'd heard about the practice as an appropriate medical procedure. I hadn't been impressed with the condition of the hospital since I arrived. Just to the left of the swinging doors to the unit there was a kitchen, of all things. What kind of a hospital has a kitchen in its intensive care unit? David's room was lit like a mortuary, and the surroundings resembled a bedroom rather than a high-tech medical facility. In fact, the entire hospital didn't look like an American hospital, and it didn't smell like one either. His physician could barely speak English, and he was pronouncing David's name wrong. He pronounced it "Dahveed," overemphasizing the *ee* sound. The doctor's terrible elocution made him sound stupid. He also sported a wild goatee and uncombed hair. I wished Gena were with me. As a nurse, she would've known the right questions to ask. About all I could do was nod my head and look convinced.

"Why is he in a coma?" I pressed.

"The coma is for David to rest. We do not want agitation or David to be uncomfortable. This can cause pain and the pressure in his brain to rise," he said.

I peered quizzically at a tiny paper cup taped to the top of David's head. A thick, white electrical wire snaked out from under the cup and connected to a monitor above the bed. There were numbers on the monitor that were rising and falling by fractions of degrees. "What's this for?" I asked him, pointing to the cup.

"We have drilled a hole in David's skull and inserted a special instrument. This measures the pressure in David's brain. The wire is plugged into the monitor, and the numbers tell us when the pressure in his brain is rising or falling."

I lifted the edge of the cup and peered at the instrument protruding out of David's skull. It resembled a steel bolt. The hole around the bolt was soaked in iodine and dried blood. The cup seemed a crude device, considering its purpose was to protect the bolt from getting jostled or dislodged from David's skull.

The doctor shifted to the foot of the bed. He carefully lifted the blanket covering David's left leg. Three steel rods nearly a quarter inch in diameter pierced straight through his thigh. No bandages covered the holes where the rods punctured the skin. The rods were hooked to cables extending toward his feet. The cables circled around a wheel-like contraption mounted to the foot of the bed, and then were secured by weights hanging near the floor. Nausea overwhelmed me as I looked up at David's face, searching for signs of discomfort. He was completely unaware that his leg was shattered.

The doctor continued his synopsis. "We cannot operate on David's leg until he is stable. The weights will keep the bones at the fracture point separated until we can realign his leg."

My mind wandered for a moment . . . I imagined the grille of a car snapping David's leg at the thigh, instantly folding him across the hood of the car and ricocheting him through the air.

I asked the most important question I could think of, which, in retrospect, probably sounded stupid. "Can he feel anything?"

"If David was awake, he would be very uncomfortable. The pain would cause the pressure in his brain to increase, and we must prevent this from happening. A normal reading on the monitor is 60.0. Any amount over this number is registering abnormally high pressure, which could cause brain damage."

I stared at the monitor that was now reading in the lower 90s, afraid to ask exactly how much damage was occurring.

The monitor wasn't the only lifeline David was attached to. He was on a ventilator to help him breathe. He had two IVs. The first IV pumped nutritional fluids into his right foot, and the second pumped medications into his right hand. Different-colored wires were attached to an electrocardiogram and fell like spaghetti noodles over his pillow, around his head, and underneath the blanket. I pulled the blanket back and found the ends of the wires attached to gummy-like circular fasteners, which were stuck all over his chest. The lines on the electrocardiogram zigzagged up and down, representing his erratic heart rate. I could only think the worst . . .

Later that evening, after spending hours by his side, a nurse escorted me to a room at the far end of the hall, where I collapsed on a foam mattress on the floor. I didn't leave the hospital for several days. The kitchen would come in handy to store and eat all the food my fellow soldiers were starting to bring me. I was beginning to understand why the intensive care unit resembled a home more than a hospital. Children who are a breath away from death need the comfort of family and friends by their side. They recuperate faster when the aromas of home-cooked meals are wafting down the hallway.

I spent those first days at David's bedside or walking the cold, empty hallways of the hospital. When by his side, I spoke words of comfort to him, but he was deaf to my entreaties. Mostly, I just looked intently at his engorged head and wallowed in my gloomy thoughts.

I glanced at the intracranial pressure monitor after what seemed to be every other breath I saw him inhale. If water doesn't boil when you're glaring at the pot, neither does the pressure in a brain disappear when you most want it to. Like electrified blood, the numbers the ICP monitor displayed registered in digitized red digits. The numbers were a guiding light of hope when they dropped but signaled a flare of despair when they rose. On occasion, David would stir and tug at his fractured leg. Sometimes he would manage a barely audible moan. These events triggered the ICP to shoot up into the high 90s, prompting the alarm to scream *bleep, bleep, bleep!* The nurses would rush in, swarm around his jerking torso, and work their magic until he settled comfortably back into his coma.

April second, nineteen eighty-three, at sometime during the day I came into existence. I was born in what is now a laundry room on the campus of a Seventh-day Adventist university, where my parents went to school and were married and soon had me. My dad was studying to be a pastor, my mom a nurse, but my dad enlisted in the army.

David was born in a self-service laundry facility—actually, it was previously an apartment at the end of a row of five apartments where Gena and I once lived while in college, but the apartment was later converted into a laundry after we graduated.

When Gena was pregnant with David, we were in our sophomore year. We barely had enough to eat, much less the extra cash for first-rate prenatal care done by a real physician at a hospital. I remember at one point we had nothing more to eat than milk and an old pumpkin caving in on itself in the fridge. Another time, we ate nothing but beans, popcorn, and Indian fry bread for weeks on end, with no decent meal to look forward to except the weekly church potluck. I learned way back that if you're eating pumpkin rinds, you're starving, and how that gnawing feeling in your stomach can motivate a person to finish getting a decent education. Anyway, we used a midwife for David's birth instead, which back then was a popular and inexpensive alternative to bringing a child into the world. Besides, Gena and I were determined and looking forward to having David at home in a more natural setting. We just didn't anticipate at the time that his infamous birthplace would later be filled with coin-operated washers, dryers, and snowflakes made of floating lint.

At his birth there were . . . complications. Gena went into labor on April Fools' Day. She had dilated only two centimeters over the course of a twenty-four-hour period. The midwife was with Gena through most of these hours, but Gena's labor was progressing so slowly that on April 2, the midwife decided to run a few errands, promising to return shortly. As soon as she left, Gena dilated from two to ten centimeters in just over an hour. As she lay writhing on the bed, she began expressing words and phrases the likes of which I'd never heard before. I was terrified! These were the days before cell phones, and I had no way of getting ahold of the midwife. With a mere ten minutes left to spare, the midwife returned and delivered our beautiful baby boy. But something was wrong. David had all his toes and fingers, he was breathing steadily, but he was too tiny! He looked like a frail old man with crinkly skin and no butt. I hastily wrapped him in a towel, laid him on the front seat of our Datsun, and rushed him to the hospital. Once there, a nurse weighed him, and he topped in at a meager three pounds eleven ounces.

Over the next few weeks after his birth, David had no further complications. We wanted to bring him home, but the hospital personnel were advising us that David needed to weigh five pounds before we could enjoy that privilege. We visited him as often as we could and spent many hours trying to get him to swallow the high-calorie formula the unit was supplying. His intake was measured in grams, not ounces. (I often cheated in making sure he drank more than his fill. When he was too full to drink any more I'd squeeze a bit more milk out of the bottle into the burp rag draped over my shoulder.) Day by day, the grams we were squirting into his mouth were being converted into ounces of fat, and his old-man wrinkles began to disappear into his plump skin. When he was just shy of five pounds, we decided to sign him out of the hospital anyway, which was our right to do—or so we were initially told. No sooner had we arrived at our apartment when an officer knocked on the door and convinced me that there would be serious judicial repercussions if I didn't get David back to the hospital right away. Since neither Gena nor I could raise David while sitting in a prison cell, we drove him back to the hospital. Then we waited another week until David weighed a few more ounces and it was all right with the state of Texas for us to have our son.

A few of the faculty members at my church-run university called David a miracle baby. I shared similar sentiments at the time, but my perspective these days has long been altered. When his sister, Dana, entered the world a few years later, she weighed even less: three pounds four ounces. I suppose twenty years ago there were many complications with premature infants. Babies who were born at three pounds and survived must have seemed tiny enough to qualify as miracles. I don't believe in miracles these days, but

I was thankful for modern medicine nevertheless, because it provided both of my underweight children the care and technical expertise that permitted them to thrive despite their low birth weights.

I see David in my memories running now—flying, really—through the open front door of our apartment back at school. His feet are not even touching the sidewalk. His blond baby curls are swept backward by the wind, and he's got a huge grin on his face. He was such a happy kid! I glance at the monitor above the hospital bed for the hundredth time that morning. Fortunately, at this moment, the numbers hover just below the point where the alarm goes off. How many brain cells will die this hour?

One day David was crawling, and the next day he was walking. He was eleven months old when he took his first step. I never saw him fall once while making the transition from crawling on all fours to walking on two feet. No kidding. He was like a newborn gazelle that just gets up and starts running from the get-go. Smart too. He knew the primary colors before his first birthday.

We had the alphabet on our refrigerator. Remember the colored letters with the magnets on the back? We were teaching David how to spell and read. I spelled out the word *water* for him one day with the letters, but I thought he was too young to understand the connection that letters have to the sounds that come out of his mouth. He came running toward me a few days later, screaming, "Daddy, I spilled the water on the floor!" I went into the kitchen to see what kind of mess he'd gotten himself into. He showed me where he pulled the letters off the fridge and threw them on the floor, which in his mind meant he had spilled water onto the floor!

We bought a set of The Bible Story books shortly after he was born. The series used to be popular and were in nearly every physician's office. I sold the books along with other religious books door-to-door one summer in Arlington, Texas. I remember this well because it was the summer we couldn't even afford a battery for my lime-green Datsun Honey Bee. I always had to park the piece of junk on a hill so I could get it rolling and then pop the clutch to get it started. So when I drove the clunker up to Arlington every day, I had to be really selective and pick the right neighborhoods that had steep hills. David loved the books and still does to this day. Now a grown man, he will find one of these books and read it just about every time he eats at the dining room table. It's a compulsive thing he'll probably do until his last meal.

There was a lovely park with a pond across the street from our college apartment. As a family, we spent a lot of time there, especially around sunset and on the weekends. David liked to feed the resident ducks and geese.

One of the photographs I took of David with my Minolta 35mm camera is of him holding out a piece of bread to a white goose. The goose was as tall as David and was rearing up on its webbed feet with its head cocked back like it was ready to take off David's arm. Those geese were mean. I came to David's rescue by chasing the squawking monstrosity all the way back to the pond.

David used to say he was going to be a weed-whacker man when he grew up. The university had a grounds crew that maintained the lawns around our apartment complex. I worked on the grounds department for a few years making less than three bucks an hour, (which explains the decaying pumpkin in the fridge). David was fascinated with the groundskeeper who used the weed whacker to trim the high grass. The groundskeeper was trimming along the sidewalk of the apartments one afternoon with the motor screaming wide open. He came around the corner and scared the hell out of David. Somehow David got it in his head that being a weed-whacker man was just what he wanted to do in life. I told David then that there were other things in life he could aspire to become, but as I waited by his bedside for him to awaken, I would've settled for him becoming the weed-whacker man of his dreams.

While he was still learning how to talk, David would tell a friend of mine that he'd already been to college. What he remembered was that he was certainly at a college when he was a child, but it was his parents who were actually attending. I guess he put two and two together and thought he'd already earned an education.

David's not waking up, and I'm rambling, I realized. *We're reliving old times here, David. Wake up! Why won't you wake up?*

Then I changed my mind.

David, don't wake up. I don't want you to start twitching and moaning again like a mummy in a horror flick. If this happens, I'll feel your pain and the alarm will go off and the nurses will flood into the room with that distraught look on their faces, and they'll start prodding you and pumping oxygen into you and speaking to you with endearing tones as though you were their son and not mine.

Don't you like the GI Joes I brought you? I've curled one under the fingers of your left hand. Why doesn't your left hand work? This GI Joe is one of the new models. Don't ask me which one, because I brought all of the new models and positioned them all over your bed. You have a whole company of soldiers manning their post and keeping an eye on you. They are here to protect you from all of the bad forces in life. One of them is even rappelling down the cable attached to your butchered leg. Know what? If you wake up, I promise to buy you every toy in the commissary. But you have to wake up.

Can you wake up for me now?

CHAPTER 5

When Hope Fails

*W*hat kinds of thoughts torment a mother's mind when she's racing to the bedside of her firstborn son and doesn't know whether he'll live or die before she gets there?

My return trip to Germany had been expedited because the Red Cross secured back-to-back commercial flights for me from Montana to New York to Frankfurt. I was at David's bedside in less than twenty-four hours after the accident. The trip would take Gena about four days. After my father dropped me off at the airport in Great Falls, it took them two days to drive back to Oak Harbor. When they got there, Gena packed our bags, grabbed her passport, took a flight out of Seattle the next day, and arrived in Frankfurt the following day. These were the days before cell phones. The last update I'd given Gena via pay phone was that the physicians were not certain whether David would survive.

Dealing with David's accident might have been more bearable if we had been together as a family. It seemed a cruel twist of fate that all of us were kept from each other by space and circumstance. My father was in Washington, I was at the hospital in Germany with David, Gena was on a plane over the Atlantic, and my mother was taking care of our daughter, Dana, at our apartment in Frankfurt. I was elated when Gena finally arrived, because she took over in ways that only a mother could.

I see her now like it was yesterday, bathing David as though she knew her touch would bring him back to life . . . She rinsed out a cotton cloth in a pail of warm, soapy water, and slowly lifted the cloth up to David's plump, round face. An oily substance oozed from David's eyelashes, an ointment the nurses had been using to lubricate his eyes while he was in his coma. Gena tenderly dabbed the cloth along his lashes until they were clean. His eyes were bulging underneath his eyelids, but they were motionless. Gena moved the washcloth over the profile of his face, and then ever so gently she pushed the cloth down and around the back of his neck as far as she could reach without aggravating his wounds. I pulled back the thin blanket covering his chest and folded it over his lower torso. His frame was tiny, dwarfed by the size of his swollen head. His bony ribs rose and fell with each laborious breath. Gena dabbed the cloth across his chest, carefully avoiding the maze of electrical wires and the patches securing the wires to his skin. She picked up his limp arm. Lifting it toward the sky, she stroked the cloth over his elbow and up to his shoulder.

"How are you doing, David?" she asked softly. "Does that feel good? My, you need a bath."

I grabbed the pail of soapy water, and we moved to the other side of the bed. I wondered what little children dream about when they're in a coma.

I remember our dog ripping another dog open while taking her for a walk. I remember Bobby, the biggest thief I ever met. I remember eating apples and going to a place where my dad could play on a drum set and a person named Josh who worked there and was friends with my dad. The room had a drum set and was padded with foam triangles. I remember Christmas at Aunt Cheryl's house and uncovering dinosaur bones in a small clay kit watching Goonies during the day and eating pee soup at mealtime. I remember orientation at first grade and my teacher Mr. Campbell, and the day that changed my life.

We had a German shepherd in Frankfurt, Sheeba, which David tried to ride like a horse. Like all shepherds, Sheeba was temperamental. She got away from us one day when we were walking her in the park and attacked a toy poodle. She made a mad dash over a distance of fifty meters, and in one sweeping motion she plucked that poodle off the ground and punctured its lungs while shaking it side to side like a stuffed animal. That horrible visual will be stuck in David's mind forever. Mine too. Thankfully, the poodle survived.

Bobby was a kid who lived in the apartments directly across the parking lot from our building. I guess Bobby stole a lot of things, and David had enough sense to understand he was turning into a no-good thief.

I took David to the music room often. The room was in my army brigade's activity center in Höchst, the suburb of Frankfurt where I was stationed. I'd practice drumming for hours while David played with Josh, an expatriate who hated a lot of things about America but worked for the US government anyway. For lunch, Josh sometimes ate a can of tuna with a plastic fork.

Cheryl is Gena's sister. She and her ex-husband happened to be stationed in Augsburg, Germany, when we were stationed in Frankfurt. We would occasionally drive down to Augsburg on the Autobahn to visit them. I drove a Buick Regal that we shipped from the states. The Buick had a digital dashboard. When I flipped a switch, the speedometer changed from miles per hour to kilometers per hour. The speedometer topped out around 130 kmh, which is pretty much what it read all the way down to Augsburg. Yet, even at this speed, it felt like we were crawling, because I often had to pull into the slow lane to let other cars pass. Every once in a while a motorcycle would fly by reaching speeds that must have been pushing 200 kmh.

David would also remember eating pea soup, apparently because it tasted like pee to him. It's one of the few words I've seen him misspell. And he'd recall his teacher Mr. Campbell on the day that changed his life.

I want to believe David was thinking happy thoughts while in his coma, but he recalls nothing but dead blackness. His memory of life before the accident is fragmented. He was young, however, so I expect him to have difficulty remembering events that transpired twenty years ago. I'm surprised he can still recall many of his friends' names and the things he once did back in the days before the accident.

Some experts say that our personalities are formed during infancy and up to age six. I'm not an expert in the field of child psychology, but if this is accurate, then David was born twice. I have memories of the kind of person he was before the accident at age six and live with the memories and realities of the person he would become. He was born on April 2, 1983 but we also celebrate his rebirth on October 12, 1989, the day of the accident. It's like we have two sons, the son who was born to us and the estranged lad who emerged

Picking Wings Off Butterflies

after the accident. But the differences in these two Davids are blurry and at times indistinguishable. It's not like there was one David one day and a different David the next. It's more like there's some semblance in our second David to the first David. When I think about the person he is now, there are times in which the characteristics of our original son pop into my awareness. These events play out like flashbacks to me, as though I am watching a scratched DVD version of his life. As he grows older, the flashbacks have become more pronounced, presumably because David's mind is still in the process of healing back to his original self. Yet we will likely always have to fill in our dreams of what David might have become through our imaginations. Most painful for me as a father is that I remember the potential I saw in David's future before the accident and the expectations that I settle for today.

If left up to me, I'd make sure that children would not be subjected to experiencing the horrors of life. Someone should nudge them away from danger when they're about to step into harm's way. There should be a mechanism in place—a default switch for fate—that prevents the cars that are going to hit them from starting. Actually, any intervention from the cosmos, which might alter the random role of cause and effect, would suffice. The woman who plowed her car into David could have been delayed by a red light. Just moments before impact, David and his friend could have stopped for a few minutes to play on the schoolyard swings. Perhaps they might have even given chase to a butterfly, which just moments before had alighted from its cocoon and was fluttering towards a new life. Because we all know how fascinating butterflies are to little boys! Any kind of delay could have shaved thirty seconds off the time it took David to walk from the school to that busy street.

Children should be prevented from experiencing any kind of trauma. They should be immune to all diseases. They should never go hungry. They should have loving families, a cozy home, plenty of animal crackers and pancakes to eat, and a comfortable bed to sleep in. They should have clothes to keep them warm and shoes to protect their delicate feet. Children should not be allowed to experience terror, grief, fear, or all the other evils that prevent them from knowing happiness. Children should only laugh and never cry. They should be wrapped in a forcefield of protection.

While I'm standing on this box . . . corn and rice should grow in places like Sudan and Darfur. Tornadoes, floods, hurricanes, tsunamis, and earthquakes should not be allowed to wreak havoc. Spearheads, guns, cannons, and nuclear bombs should never have been invented. Madmen should not be allowed to rule. People should not be subjected to tyranny. Prisons should not exist. Nice guys should finish first. A pill should be invented that kills AIDS and another pill that cures cancer. And there has got to be a way to help people with Alzheimer's remember their names and who loves them. When our brains get sick, there should be a store where we can buy a new mind. Everyone should have a roof over their heads, shoes on their feet, clothes on their backs, and food spilling out of their cupboards.

If it were up to me, I would have designed another plan for this world that did not include human misery. I could easily sketch out several possibilities on a napkin while sipping a cup of latte. But I'm only human, and supernatural conjectures are pointless.

But you'll have to pardon my philosophical ruminations. I had a lot of time to think about David's predicament as I sat by his bedside, and I've spent two decades thereafter working through my anger at the injustice of him being robbed of a normal life. And what I know is that if something created this world, *It* could have done a better job. And if something did not create this world, than we—as humans—have enough collective compassion and foresight to build a better one.

Many psychiatrists and medical professionals will testify that anger is one of the first emotions a person is likely to feel after they've experienced loss or trauma. The death of a spouse, a child, or a family member represents the most significant loss we can experience. Short of death, watching our loved ones endure physical and emotional pain will cause us to seethe with rage to the extent that we feel like we are going to explode. For many individuals, this anger is likely to be directed toward God.

Frankly, up to that moment in my life I thought I knew God. Sure, I'd never seen God and never heard Him speak, but I prayed. I'd been praying ever since I could kneel beside my bed as a toddler and fold my hands. I always understood my conversations with God were one-sided, and I was fine with that. But as I sat at David's bedside, what I really needed was His intervention. *Will God now intervene on David's behalf?* I wondered. *And if God intervenes now, then why didn't He intervene before the moment of impact?* These questions begged for answers. We ask questions such as these not to place blame on God, but because we want to understand the basic truths about how and why things happen to us, and whether there are things we can do to control the events that occur in our lives. Ultimately, what we really want to know, is what is real and truthful. What we do not want to believe, is in ideas that simply give us false hope.

Perhaps it's a good thing, however, that children aren't asking themselves these kinds of questions when they're six years old. Children don't ask these grown-up questions, because they're not even aware these are questions worth asking. What children do is survive. They focus on the prize of living, and if it is within their power, they pull through. Death is not an option when death is an unknown. Their little minds, free of philosophical innuendos, press on with optimism. Since I was receiving no direct responses from God, facing reality and trying to be optimistic about it were my only options.

A week passed, and there was only one noticeable sign of David's improvement: he survived. His condition was stable, but he was still in a coma. The ICP monitor was registering slightly lower numbers, but the numbers were still high, averaging in the upper 70s. Perhaps I was being too hopeful, but I could swear David was trying to wake up. He was growing more fidgety as the days went on, and more medication was required to keep him comatose.

A different doctor visited and gave us an update. Her English was better, and she confirmed my suspicions. "David is becoming more agitated, but we must still give him medicine to help him sleep. Tomorrow we will take David in for surgery to operate on his leg."

"What will you do to his leg?" I asked, wondering if David would have full use of his leg after they operated.

"We will have to pull his leg apart to separate the fracture and then reset the break in his femur. We will also have to add support, since the break is severe," she said. "We'll do this by attaching steel plates to his thighbone with screws."

This sounded like it was going to cause David a lot of pain for a long time.

"How long do you plan on inducing the coma?" Gena asked.

"Perhaps a few more weeks. He still has high levels of pressure in his brain."

"Do you think he's going to have permanent brain damage?" I asked.

Her face offered no indication of optimism. Her reply was blunt. "We did an initial test of David's brain when he first arrived. The test showed serious trauma."

I pressed for details.

"We sent electrical impulses into David's brain to measure reaction times," she explained. "There was a significant gap in the time it took his brain to register the signals. There are also a few bruised areas in his brain indicating permanent damage."

The doctor showed us X-rays of David's brain. She pointed to dark spots in the frontal lobe area and another spot deep in the center near the hypothalamus.

"Those areas won't heal, will they?" Gena asked.

"It's possible, but too early to tell. Children, especially young children, can heal rapidly. Older people have more difficulty. If there are areas that are damaged, the brain can sometimes rewire itself and make new connections. David might be able to relearn functions that may be damaged."

I wondered what parts of David wouldn't be working when he awakened. Would he have memory loss? Would he be able to speak or walk? Would he remember me? Would he forget the mother who gave him life?

CHAPTER 6

ABOVE AND BEYOND THE CALL OF DUTY

The army can be a heartless organization. It's not in the business of enhancing personal relationships and catering to the needs of the family unit. Its goal will always be the mission, and the mission can only be accomplished by soldiers who are detached from the distractions of everyday family life.

Then again, individual soldiers can be surprisingly compassionate.

I was summoned to battalion headquarters about a week after David's accident, and the major was resolute as to what I must do. I was ordered to man my post. The post assigned to me was the hospital. I was put in charge of looking after only one individual: my son.

The major's wife had baked our family a spinach quiche. Wearing his camouflage battle dress uniform and spit-shined boots, he handed the quiche to me as we stood in his

Picking Wings Off Butterflies

office punctuated with flags and army paraphernalia. I didn't know whether to salute him or hug him but erred on the side of protocol. He informed me that his wife had personally taken on the assignment of ensuring that my family was not troubled with making food rations for the foreseeable future. Within a short period of time, we received more foodstuffs than we could possibly consume from individuals I never knew and would never meet. Provisions piled up on the kitchen table at the hospital and filled the refrigerator in our apartment.

Days were passing in a blur. The intensive care unit became our second home. The unit didn't have any kind of a visitors' area or lobby, so we took over the kitchen area as though it were our own place of refuge. The nurses, Dalia and Stephanie, made sure we were comfortable, but it was difficult to communicate with them due to the language barrier. They brought us many steaming cups of tea. We became familiar with a few of the children being treated in the rooms down the hall. I remember one young girl who had fallen off her bicycle. She was well on her way to recovery. Her mother visited often, and as she read to her daughter, the Germanic words of the story echoed through the corridor. I didn't understand the words, but the story must have been sweet, as revealed in the mother's endearing tone.

Another two weeks passed, and then one day David's eyes slipped open like seeds cracking to life: a half-open right eye with the left eye opening just a sliver. His eyelids seemed heavy as though glued shut by the translucent ointment. His pupils darted back and forth, but he could barely move his head. Gena leaned over his bed to face him, and he recognized her! I waited for him to say, "Hi, Mom!" but his lips parted with nothing but silence. Instead, his eyes indicated what he wanted to say. They said, *I don't know what's happening and where I'm at, but I'm glad you're here.*

"Hey, big boy! You're awake. You've been asleep for a long time, over three weeks. Can you believe it? We've missed you," Gena said.

"Where have you been, David? Have you been dreaming? You're in the hospital. You're going to be okay," I said.

His head turned ever so slightly as he looked in the direction of our voices, and his fingers twitched as he tried to shift his torso out of the crevasse his little body had formed in the bed.

"Can you move your feet?" I asked.

No reaction. Either he could not move his legs or my request wasn't registering in his brain.

A few days passed, and the fog that clouded his mind seemed to be dissipating. I measured his progress in his smiles. It was as though his face had frozen in the coma and was beginning to thaw. When he smiled, the right corner of his mouth trembled upward and his right eyelid lifted ever so slightly. If you didn't know David, you might not have guessed he was smiling. But we knew his face, and I'm telling you, he was smiling!

The left side of his face, however, hung lifeless as though its muscles were still frozen in a permanent frown. This was especially noticeable during the moments I joked with him, trying to get him to laugh. The right side of his face would light up, the corner of his mouth rising as it should, even exposing his teeth, but the left side of his mouth remained unresponsive.

To his credit, I'm surprised he even felt like smiling at all. He had good reason to look miserable. When he tugged on the bolts running through his leg, he'd grimace with pain. When he moved his hands and arms, he discovered he was pinned down like the fairy-tale giant Gulliver, but secured with electrical wires instead of ropes. When the pain got too unbearable, he'd twitch and tug any way he could, the alarms would beep loudly, and the nurses would rush in and pump him with another dose of morphine.

We encouraged David as best we could by telling him everything was going to be all right. We told him he'd been in a serious accident, he'd banged his head, and this was the reason he felt so confused. We kept secret the details regarding his head injuries, because we didn't know the specifics yet. What we knew was that some processes were not functioning in his brain. How much he understood, I don't know. I suspect he was just beginning to recognize that his mind was no longer working like it used to work.

I remember waking up to a doctor drawing my blood and my dad rolling me down the halls in the hospital while I ate Teddy Grahams. That was the first time I ate those and I like them even today. I remember waking up in my bed and hearing people on the other side of the curtain. I remember my dad had gotten me every GI Joe ever made. My dad comes up with a box and dumps the GI Joes all over me on my bed.

I had lifted the cardboard box full of tiny GI Joes above David's stomach as he lay on his hospital bed one afternoon. He got a kick out of me dumping them all over him and grinned from ear to ear—sort of. The toys covered his waist and legs, but a few tumbled onto the floor. I picked up the figurines one by one and put them in his right hand so he could check them out. He looked at the front packaging to see who the Joes were, and I'd flip the package over so he could read their statistics.

He started whispering about a week after he came out of

his coma. He was talking! You'd think he was yelling by the way he filled his lungs and forced the words out. I had to lean over his bed to hear what he was trying to say. The words came out raspy and flat with no inflection or tone. And talking wore him out. It was as if he had only enough energy to speak a dozen words a day. This limited his vocabulary to words and phrases such as *yes, no, I'm hungry, I'm tired,* and *it hurts.*

Once he started whispering, he also got more fidgety. His mind was telling him it was time to get on with life, yet his body wasn't cooperating. We'd crank up the old hospital bed and support his head with pillows so he wouldn't flop over. This was a minor ordeal, what with all the wires and tubes holding him down. We had to check to see that we hadn't unplugged all the wires coming from the EKG, make sure he wasn't pinching any of his IV lines, and then carefully shove more pillows under his broken leg. When we repositioned him, his arms would jerk about in spasmodic gestures like a newborn infant. More than once he tried to rip the IV needles out of his arms. And he was obsessed with that stupid cup taped to his head, clawing away at it in frantic attacks, but only managing to scratch his forehead.

The numbers on the ICP monitor had been progressively dropping since the first week. The numbers still hadn't settled into the normal range, but his physician felt comfortable that the pressure in his brain was no longer a threat.

For the first time, I heard optimism in her voice. "We are very surprised at David's recovery."

"It was serious, wasn't it?" I asked without expecting an answer. I was genuinely proud of how hard David had fought to survive and how far he had come.

"His recovery has been amazing," she said.

"Will he have permanent brain damage?" I asked.

"He will have lingering problems—"

"But he'll be all right?" I asked.

"David's head injuries are serious. He has damage that will be with him for the rest of his life. But he's still young. He's really progressed in the past weeks, and we're hopeful the damage has not affected important areas," she said.

I didn't want to hear this crap. The fact was David survived. His recovery was remarkable—like he was unstoppable. Sure, he was only whispering, but his voice was getting stronger. He seemed less confused and more coherent every day. He could read the information on the back of the GI Joe packaging, couldn't he? He was responding to our questions and laughing at my jokes—right? Although he was still in a world of hurt, we could see his old self coming back to life.

Delusion has its merits. As much as I wanted to believe he was getting well, I couldn't overlook the obvious. David's left arm was virtually useless. When we spoke to him, he had a glassy-eyed expression. Instructions weren't registering. He had the vocabulary of a toddler. There was a clear distinction between what the right side of his face was expressing as opposed to the left side of his face—and who wants to go through life with half their face not working? His left leg was a fractured mess held together with metal planks and bolts. The fracture would heal, but there was a real possibility that he would never be able to walk or run.

CHAPTER 7

SAUERKRAUT NEVER TASTED SO GOOD

A nurse pushing a wheelchair popped into David's room and asked with a thick accent, "Hallo, David. Are you hungry?"

"Yes," he grunted, with the biggest half smile I'd seen to date. The kid hadn't eaten for over three weeks!

Another nurse joined her at David's bedside. They rolled his covers back and began the arduous task of unplugging the web of wires encircling him. They carefully lifted him out of bed and set him in the wheelchair. His body started to fall forward, and they quickly shoved pillows around his rib cage to prop him up. Then they strapped a makeshift table onto the wheelchair, turning it into a rolling high chair of sorts. As they wheeled him toward the door, he had a puzzled look on his face.

I watched his eyes track from side to side as he passed through the doorway. I imagined his brain was recording the event similar to how a camera might film a scene lit by a strobe light. David was catching only part of the action. He appeared dizzy, even nauseated. The nurse pushing his chair stopped in the hallway just outside the kitchen door and spun David around so he was staring down the length of the hallway. From the corner of his eye, he saw the nurse walk into the kitchen but missed the part when she came back. Suddenly, he noticed the food the nurse had placed in front of him, but he was unaware that she was trying to get him to hold a fork. Once he grabbed the fork, he appeared to have forgotten why he was grabbing it, until the nurse redirected his attention to the food. David seemed shocked when he finally noticed his first meal in weeks. I thought they'd serve him Jell-O or a bowl of Rocky Road ice cream. Instead, they offered him a plateful of sauerkraut garnished with bratwurst!

Gripping the fork like a baby chimpanzee, he took a stab at the stringy, smelly cabbage. The fork tines jabbed the table about four inches to the right of the plate. *Something's wrong*, I thought. His hand-eye coordination was way off target. He tried again with the same result and fidgeted with frustration. He stabbed frantically at the food a few more times but kept forking the table. The nurse helped him by sliding the plate over. He managed to scoop a few strands of sauerkraut onto the fork and aimed for his lips. By twisting his head, he was able to land the sour morsels into his mouth. He reacted to the taste with disgust. Nothing abnormal there!

"Is that good?" I asked him.

He wasn't in the mood for chitchat. His stomach had a hole in it, and he couldn't care less about what was sliding down his throat to fill the void.

His arm moved back and forth like a pendulum. I

could have set my watch to its rhythm. He was stabbing the plate at exactly the same spot every time. Sometimes he managed to get a few morsels of sauerkraut on the fork, and sometimes he came up empty. Even so, he kept repeating the pattern—reach, stab, lift, bite—over and over again. About the only thing we could do to help was to keep moving the pile of sauerkraut to where he found the food the last time he stabbed it.

I thought it would be fun to pull a practical joke on him. While he was putting the fork to his mouth, I moved the plate four inches out of the way. The fork stabbed the table as though he still thought the plate was in the same spot, but he didn't stop. He moved the fork back up to his mouth and attempted to eat the air. Then he tried again to stab more food and hit the same empty target. Again, he moved the fork to his mouth as though it had food on it.

I was sickened by what I saw. I knew his coordination was off, but his sense of awareness to his surroundings was disturbingly out of whack. It was as if his world had shifted four inches since the accident, and he didn't have a clue it had moved. I recalled the doctor telling me weeks earlier that there was a delay in the way David's brain was processing signals, and I now understood that it might take years—or a lifetime—for him to get back to being normal, if indeed he would ever be normal.

In the coming days, David would enjoy eating more than platefuls of sauerkraut, and he didn't care what kind of grub he was served. Somebody had to devour all the food my fellow soldiers were bringing us. Like a ravenous pig, he'd eat everything we put in front of him. As the days went by, his aim got better, but eating was still a ritual for him, requiring a great deal of concentration. Once he sat down to the task of eating, though, he was all business.

He also started laughing again. In the movie *Forrest Gump*, Forrest's mother is determined that her son be treated like a normal child, and getting Forrest a good education is her top priority. But the school principal doesn't share her determination. Since Forrest's entrance test score is below normal by five points, Forrest will have to be placed in a special school. The principal implies that Ms. Gump can persuade him not to place Forrest in a special school if she has sex with him. In the next scene, Forrest is sitting on a swing under a tree in front of the Southern mansion where he and his mother live. In the background, we hear the grunts of the principal having sex with Forrest's mother in a second-floor bedroom. Moments later, the principal walks through the front door and Forrest is now sitting on a rocking chair on the front porch. The principal wipes his brow and tells Forrest how much his mother cares about his schooling. Forrest turns to him and grunts, "He, he, he, he, he," mimicking the sounds he's just overheard. That's the sound David made when he laughed, monotonous and whispery.

Not only would David learn how to laugh again, but more importantly, he'd find his voice. After he found his voice, he picked up a delightfully embarrassing habit. When he couldn't find the proper terminology to make complete sentences, he'd use cuss words to get his point across. Not the tame cuss words Grandma might have used like *darn* and *poppycock*, but words better suited to enliven prison talk.

"Did you get enough to eat, David?" the nurse asked.

"Yeah, fucking good."

"The nurse is going to give you a bath now, David," Gena said to him.

"That shitty nurse there?"

"That one," I reply.

"But the goddamn water is fucking cold!"

I asked the physician about this distasteful phenomenon.

"It's caused by David's frontal lobe damage. He's more impulsive, and he'll have less control in the future over what he's saying."

In the coming years, I'd learn more about the complexities of the human brain. I'd discover that various parts of the brain control certain functions, that many brain functions are carried out through neurotransmitters assisted by electrical impulses and chemicals, and that all of these components somehow mesh together to form a person's personality. At the time, I was ignorant of these complexities, but from what the doctor was telling me, David's brain had been affected by the accident in different ways. I assumed the accident caused temporary brain damage, which meant, given time, the damage would heal itself and David would get well. What I discovered was that David's head injuries would not only cause parts of his body not to function, but these injuries would also cause drastic changes to his personality. In effect, as his brain was rewiring itself with new pathways, these physical changes were altering the processes and outcomes of his thoughts—in other words, his mental state of being, his very nature. It was becoming more apparent that the boy I knew from infancy to age six would not be the same boy throughout the rest of his life.

Would I love the new David as much as the old David? Of course I would. If David's personality changed, it would not alter the love I have for him. It's not really an option for parents to love or not love their children. This kind of love is hardwired into our genes through tens of thousands of years of evolved human behavior. Would I like the new David? This was the pivotal question.

Did I like the new way David had learned to express

himself that resembled a vulgar lunatic? Given David's zombie-like eating habits, would I be embarrassed to take him out in public to eat? Whether David could walk again was still uncertain. Would I enjoy spending the rest of my life hand carrying him to and from his wheelchair to wherever he felt like sitting? Would I enjoy spending the rest of my life driving David to various therapies and other appointments? Would Gena and I continue to like taking care of David for the rest of our lives, given that caring for him would entail drastic changes to our lifestyle and force us to put our personal goals on hold indefinitely? After all, parents are people too. We have aspirations and dreams. We have ideas about where we see ourselves in five, twenty, and thirty years down the road. Loving David was easy, but did I like being confronted with the alternative: that I could be taking care of David for the rest of his life—my life? And I would never, ever be able to live my own life as I had planned.

When people get married and have children, they expect to make compromises. Most couples are willing to make concessions because of the obvious reason that having someone to share your life with is a source of immense joy. Even better, raising children with a life partner is a marvelous wonder of the human experience. This pleasure is so satisfying that many parents are willing to disregard their own happiness to ensure that their children succeed and enjoy life.

Reality, however, does not always measure up to the ideal. Raising children is hard work, and most people expect that at some point their responsibilities as parents will end. Like chicks and cubs in the animal kingdom, there is a natural timeline in which the young are reared to an age at which they can take care of themselves, the time when they are affectionately—and merrily—kicked out of the nest or den. What parents and couples expect to be doing in the later years of their lives is rekindling their dreams and reacquainting themselves with each other. They have suspended their personal lives for roughly two decades and now feel an inherent need to complete the cycle of their lives. There is life beyond raising and caring for children. It's a good life just waiting to be explored, but it cannot be enjoyed until the youngest hatchling in the nest spreads its own wings and takes flight.

So, what happens when a member of the family is broken? What happens when the parents or siblings of a broken family member are required to forfeit their future in order to take care of a person with special needs?

What initially happens is that we look for ways to cope. And we sometimes do this by seeking a divine reason for why we seem to have been chosen to bear this enormous responsibility. And we do this for good reason, because it helps ease the burden. But even if we do not seek a divine reason for being derailed from our personal lives, it would make no difference, for as humans we have evolved to express compassion. Parent to child, lover to companion, family member to clan, citizen to country—we take care of our own, and we do so with natural affection.

Eventually, however, everyone except the saints among us will grow weary of the task. We can handle things for a time, a brief spell really, until we start thinking about our own lives again. And we'll think our wishes to return to our own lives to be selfish. Imagine—the sheer audacity of it—thinking about what *we* want as opposed to what *they* need, as though we've lost the right to think about our own future and happiness. Then comes the guilt. Then flows the feeling that we are selfish and victims of our passions and desires. I cannot tell you that overcoming these feelings is easy, only

Picking Wings Off Butterflies

that the anxiety these emotions cause is bearable. But this is only if a person accepts being human and knows that there is time to figure things out. That's the ticket. Realize you are fallible, accept that you're prone to a range of conflicting thoughts and desires, and then give yourself time to find the right balance between how much time you should spend on pursuing your own happiness and how much energy you can realistically exert helping others.

CHAPTER 8

ONE STEP AT A TIME

My transfer orders moved swiftly up the army's chain of command. David needed specialized care and an abundance of therapies the army couldn't provide in Frankfurt. I was offered two locations that could administer David's medical needs: Walter Reed Army Medical Center in Washington, DC, and Brooke Army Medical Center in San Antonio, Texas. The decision would be a comfortable one. Gena and I had gone to college in Keene, Texas, and Gena still had an active nursing license to practice there.

We left about a week later on a C-5 medical transport plane. David was wheeled up the back door ramp on a gurney surrounded by air force personnel holding his tubes, wires, and monitoring devices. The medical evacuation team and the flight crew were concerned. David was still prone to experiencing excessively high brain pressure, so they'd have to monitor him closely, as well as fly the plane lower than its normal cruising altitude. They strapped David to

Picking Wings Off Butterflies

one of a dozen cots at the rear of the plane, most of which were already filled with other patients being transported for various medical reasons, and off we flew.

Riding in a C-5 is like riding in a humming steel cocoon. The accommodations are bare-bones. The scratchy, olive, drab seats face the rear of the plane, and you have to strap yourself in with a harness similar to what you'd find in an F-16. There are no windows and nothing to look at except the cocoon's skeletal innards, with cargo rope netting dangling from the sides of the fuselage like giant spiderwebs.

A female flight attendant wearing scuffed boots offered us a blanket to keep warm and earplugs to dull the metallic hum. She later served Gena and me each a meal: a brown-box refreshment unit consisting of a sandwich, chips, a piece of fruit, and a pint of milk.

My mother, my daughter, my car, my dog, my household goods, and our lives would remain in Frankfurt until given orders of their own to be moved at a time yet to be determined. Little did we know this would all take many months.

I was young when it happened. The whole thing was like a dream state, but so much in reality that at the time it was difficult to tell whether or not it was a reality, or just something I was thinking about. I wasn't for sure what had happened to me to the extent that it happened until we got to Texas.

There's a lot of hurry up and waiting to be done in the army, but things do get done. We were taken from the plane directly to Brooke Army Medical Center. David was processed in through the ER because the medical staff at the hospital were not expecting him. I had thought they *would* be expecting him. David's condition was an ongoing emergency. All the transport preparations had been made in Frankfurt, so I thought it incomprehensible when the hospital staff in San Antonio didn't have a clue he was coming. Eventually, one of the pediatricians gave David an initial assessment. It was late afternoon by the time the physician gave David a thorough once-over, and we got him up to speed on everything that had transpired medically for David in the past month. The three of us were then driven to temporary housing located in an old, remodeled hotel on post.

The army would make up for its initial lack of preparation for David within the coming days. Our mornings started early by getting David up and into his wheelchair. There was no cafeteria or restaurant where we stayed, so we munched on what little breakfast we could get from the vending machines. Then we'd wait for the van that would take us to the hospital. Every day was different, but the first weeks were spent visiting countless specialists and undergoing innumerable tests. I didn't realize there were so many areas of specialization in the medical field. We rolled David through the doors of general practitioners, pediatricians, physical therapists, occupational therapists, neurologists, orthopedic surgeons, speech therapists, and psychologists. Each physician needed special tests to be performed in order to make their evaluations. Additional days were spent conducting these tests and waiting for specialists' reviews and reports. X-rays were done on David's leg, and CAT scans were performed on his brain.

David was a real trooper. He did his best on the tests and responded to the doctors as best he could. He was eating well. His speech was improving. The tone of his voice was still flat and guttural, but the volume was returning. The profanity he'd been using began to diminish not only

Picking Wings Off Butterflies

because we chided him for swearing but also because he was starting to remember more words and better ways of expressing himself.

To pass the time, I turned David's borrowed wheelchair into a race car, and the long hallways became our Grand Prix. I'd power slide him around corners and accelerate him down the long hallways. We had a lot of life-threatening close calls with furniture, pill carts, and the nurses who got in our way. You should have heard David hee-hawing with laughter!

Somehow, I must have gotten lost in the army's vast bureaucracy and legions of paperwork. For three weeks I had no one to report to. Nor did I feel the need to tell someone who outranked me that Sergeant Stahlecker hadn't been to work in over a month. I assumed that the transfer of my family to San Antonio had been a permanent move. After all, I was still following my original orders delivered by my superior to man my post by caring for my son.

With the reports from the specialists all in, the doctors scheduled David on a hefty regimen of therapies that included physical, occupational, and speech therapies. The locations of the therapies were housed at different buildings on the post and were scheduled all day long, five days a week. The injured, and those who tended to them, apparently rested on the weekends. We rented a car from a not-so-reputable agency. With no established credit card to cover potential incidentals, it was the only rental agency we could find that would take our cash. The agency demanded we sign a stack of paperwork and charged us a fortune for the early model, baby-blue station wagon. It was ugly, but we needed the space behind the passenger seat so we could throw in David's wheelchair.

Eventually, the army did manage to catch up to me

and issued me orders to report to an army intelligence battalion located at the Quadrangle at Fort Sam Houston near downtown San Antonio. I was assigned to work under two lieutenants and a captain and given the task of editing training manuals. The task of caring for David and taking him to his endless appointments now fell entirely on Gena.

I killed a lot of time standing at the doorway of my office, peering into the adjacent courtyard. The Quadrangle was really a bizarre place. It resembled what could only be described as a charming fortress that I presumed once stood out in the middle of the Texas countryside of yesteryear but was now surrounded by older homes on the outskirts of San Antonio. The Quadrangle reminded me of old photographs I'd seen of army posts during early American history, except it wasn't built from felled logs. The large courtyard in the center was contained by roughly four equal sides of chiseled limestone blocks. An oddly placed watchtower stood in the courtyard. Rusty old cannons and gun turrets were scattered around in the grass and under the mesquite and ash trees. What was peculiar about the fort was that it was residence to numerous peacocks and a small herd of white-tailed deer. The deer had full reign of the place and were tame enough to pet. The deer's only escape would have been through the tunnel at the main entrance, but the entrance was secured by an iron gate.

Gena and I finally scraped together enough cash to rent a dinky three-bedroom house on the east side of San Antonio only seven miles from Fort Sam Houston. We needed the space, as my mother and daughter were finally joining us. We even arranged to have Sheeba, our dog, shipped stateside, but she would not be living with us for a while. Sheeba caught a plane to Missouri instead, which was where Gena's parents were living, and they watched her until life settled down for

Picking Wings Off Butterflies

us. The poor pooch had a miserable flight. By the time she arrived in Missouri, she was covered in her own feces and vomit. After picking her up at the airport, Gena's parents hosed her down at the first rest stop outside town.

After my mother and Dana arrived, we finally had our whole family back together again, but it was presumptuous for me to conclude that because we were together life would get smoother. Cash was tight, and I was forced to return the rental car. I bought a twenty-one-speed bike to get to work. The seven-mile trip to the Quadrangle each morning began well before daybreak, weaving through the most dangerous traffic I'd ever encountered. Given that my bike was black and I was wearing camouflage clothes didn't help. After several close calls, I bought a neon-colored vest. I'm surprised I survived the daily ordeal.

Every person or thing in the army needs special orders before it can be moved an inch, but the process of moving all of my household belongings from Frankfurt got more complicated than it needed to be. David, Gena, and I were escorted out of Germany with "a purpose." This is army lingo for moving fast with a known destination. Yet, when we got to Brooke Army Medical Center, everyone was moving like pond water. This is army lingo for moving without a care in the world and thus being slow enough to stagnate. Upon our arrival, no one seemed to know that David was coming or what should be done with him. My mother and daughter followed us stateside a month later, but because the process was taking so long to get their orders to travel, we just went ahead and paid for their way on a commercial airliner so that we could be with them again. Meanwhile, my car, all our household goods, and all our personal belongings still remained in Frankfurt, and they would remain there for the next six months gathering dust.

This would have been a great time for the army to kick in extra pay. Normally, the army pays extra to compensate for personnel and their families forced to endure certain hardships. Unfortunately, there was a glitch in the payroll department, and my regular pay started getting sent to a soldier somewhere in the Northeast. While this was getting worked out, I was getting advances on my pay in an amount roughly equivalent to what my salary had been. So not only was I not getting my full salary, but I was not getting the added funds that would have allowed me to continue paying for many of the additional expenses we were incurring by moving. The most important extra expense we had was renting the car we needed to get David to his therapies. My funds were so screwed up that it would take almost a year of meetings with people in the personnel department—even after I got out of the army—to get all the pay that was due me. Needless to say, it got old sitting on the floor of our rented home eating with paper plates and plastic utensils. Riding my bike back and forth to work was not ideal, and we had to discontinue most of David's therapies until we got wheels again. Luckily, Gena's brother sold us his decrepit Toyota. The two-door coupe ran on a huge six-cylinder engine, and he'd packed the trunk full of cement blocks to keep it on the pavement when hitting the accelerator. I drove the clunker until it bit the dust a few months later while I was driving it downtown somewhere. I coasted it into a vacant lot, and a salvage company paid me $15.00 to haul it away. Lucky me.

And just as things were looking up, the army sent me back to Frankfurt! I had about three months remaining on my four-year obligation. The officers at the Quadrangle were stupefied and used what little clout they had to try and convince the powers who reigned in distant offices to let me finish my tour in Texas, but to no avail. So I said good-bye to my mom, hugged the kids, apologized to Gena for leaving her with the enormous task of taking care of David on her own, and headed back to Germany.

When I arrived at my company barracks in Frankfurt, my first sergeant had a few choice words of his own. "Stahlecker, what the hell are you doing back here?"

I was tempted to mutter a half-witted response about recently serving in an army intelligence unit, and that there were details about army intel that puzzled me, but I kept my mouth shut.

He shook his head and took a seat behind his desk. "Well, the company is in Adelsried on maneuvers for the next month. Guess you can pull guard duty back here."

And so I did. Twenty-four hours on and twenty-four off, with duty consisting of making sure nobody stole the desk I sat in front of, eating burnt microwaved popcorn, and staring down a vacated hallway, wondering how my family was surviving without me.

Unexpectedly a few weeks later, my father up and had a heart attack and nearly died. They shocked him back to life at the hospital with a defibrillator. His heart attack apparently settled the army's requirement that a soldier within its ranks was going through more stress than he needed to in a time of peace. In light of my extenuating circumstances, the army then offered me a "compassionate discharge" under honorable circumstances. All things considered, I took the offer. The irony of the discharge was that I walked away a free man just weeks before I would have completed my four-year tour anyway.

Not long after we arrived in Texas we were going about our usual business . . . mom and dad getting ready for the day. I'm watching He-Man. My mom says she'll be in the other room and leaves me to my show. I'm on the couch. My wheelchair is on the other side of the room. I start to think maybe I can walk to the wheelchair. So slowly and shakily I remember I got up and started walking and my mom came in and saw me. I think she was shocked.

David's challenges at this time were far less mundane than the ones I dealt with during my last few months in the army. I'd say they were monumental, given that he was trying to relearn how to talk, and eat, and think. But his primary objective? Apparently, it was to get up and walk.

For a normal brain, learning how to walk is instinctual. As infants, we simply watch the giant people dancing their way around us and we stand up and join them one day. For David, the established connections in his brain that once provided the instructions on how to walk had been severed. The neurons that once fired electrical signals from his brain through the intricate maze of muscles and tissues down to the tips of his toes and back would have to be reestablished. Of course, David was ignorant of how this process was all going to play out. He just had the desire to walk.

What a marvel of mental prowess this must have been for him! I was not with him in San Antonio, but I can imagine David sitting on the edge of the couch. He eyes his goal leaning against the wall across the room—that mechanical contraption with its rubbery, round, spoke-filled legs, otherwise known as the wheelchair. Perhaps he's listening to Dana outside on the porch giggling with the little girl from next door. He wants to play with them, but he can't get out the front door. He rises and braces himself on the arm of the couch. His right foot is ready for action, but his left foot feels like a dead, fleshy object, dangling and unwilling to move. And then his mind engages with determination. His left foot slides forward, surprising himself with the possibility. He leans on it, wondering if the leg will bear his weight. *Let go of the couch*, he tells himself. *If I can stand, I just might walk.* He lets go and stands! His sense of accomplishment would have been overwhelming and the anticipation of success pressing him on with the possibilities.

Can I pull it off? he wonders. But now he's wobbling. His legs have not stood for months. The limbs are apprehensive to engage. In his brain, neurons are firing, looking for old pathways and discovering that the synapses that once permitted the marvel of electrical impulses have been disconnected, or that those once-established connections now lead to darkened dead ends where his brain has been damaged. Electrical messengers are ordered by other portions of the brain to survey the damage and to ascertain whether new pathways can be remapped.

Nanoseconds pass, and while all this electrical activity is sparking, still other mental processes are engaging. David's mind is racing through emotions, and among the many emotions he's processing is his fear of falling while simultaneously clinging to hope. Perspiration is forming on his forehead. His breathing intensifies. Adrenaline rushes through his body, infusing him with the strength he will need to walk the eight feet to victory.

He leans fully on his injured leg. Sharp pain shoots up his spine as the pins and bolts that have been holding his fractured leg together slide against the bone and muscle within his thigh. But the pain is not too unbearable, and he shifts his right foot forward. Two steps! He senses how proud his mother will be. He takes a step forward with his left foot and notices it doesn't work like it used to. His heel will not connect with the floor, and he has to use his toes instead. But this throws him off balance, and as he stumbles headlong, he throws his right foot forward. With momentum now propelling him, he tiptoes—practically tripping—the rest of the way to his wheelchair. And when he arrives at his wheelchair, he realizes he won't need it anymore!

CHAPTER 9

LED ASTRAY IN HANDCUFFS

FLASHFORWARD

*D*avid is now twenty-six.

You will no doubt notice that I've abruptly skipped two decades in the timeline of David's story. Hopefully, however, you will appreciate this intrusion in the timeline, and understand why I must interrupt my recounting of the past events of his life to explain an emergency that is now unfolding in real time. This may not translate into the most polished flow of ideas, but it is the best way to express the chaos of what it's like raising a child with a traumatic brain injury. So I promise I'll get back to his road to recovery in the next chapter, just as soon as I can mentally process the latest catastrophe.

Truth be told, I had hoped I would have his book done by now, but David's story has been difficult from its inception.

It was tough enough for me to revive memories I wanted to forget. And to a certain extant, reliving burdensome events and cooking them up into entertaining anecdotes has been therapeutic, but it's all just taking a lot longer than I'd planned. Now this . . . Now, I'll have to dredge these memories up while living through what will be the beginning of the second worst period of our lives as a family.

David was arrested at his apartment in Kenai in July 2007.

I don't feel like continuing to write—really, I don't. I haven't felt much like doing anything since his arrest. Writing is for those who wish to let their spirits soar, and for the past six months, I've been spiraling downward into despair. Writing should be enjoyable; otherwise, there's not much point to it. I've always feared the worst for David, and what I have dreaded the most since his accident is that he'd have another accident worse than being hit by a car. That David could die at any time, especially given his handicaps, has been an ongoing concern. Secondary to this fear was that David could be arrested and go to prison. This was a justifiable fear considering the interest the police had taken in his life ever since they saw him stumbling down the sidewalk in St. George and surmised he was a misfit.

When I began this project, I wanted to help David tell *his* story, to breathe life into his otherwise troublesome existence. I'd further hoped that he and I could write his story together in a way that might inspire others. These would be parents with handicapped children, families who have raised children with severe head injuries, medical and other professionals needing insight into the complexities of traumatic brain injuries, teachers who might be struggling with how to better educate and integrate the "intellectually challenged" into the world, and anyone else who might gain

Picking Wings Off Butterflies

inspiration from his story. The project now seems more daunting than ever.

Frankly, I'm also embarrassed. There have never been a lot of things David's done in his life that would make me proud, and his arrest certainly isn't going to qualify. I hesitate to tell you what he stands accused of, lest you think ill of him or me. I wouldn't want you thinking I failed to teach my son how to live an honest life, or that he was a rotten egg to begin with. My concerns may seem self-centered, but I'm genuinely cautious about what people will think not only of David but also of my entire family. I've always tried to give people the benefit of the doubt, but you know how people can be. As a species, we can be downright cruel to our own kind. And speaking on behalf of my family, we've been trying hard to establish new friendships in our new community, and David's little shenanigan isn't going to help us.

Nevertheless, I find myself at a peculiar juncture where I question whether I am now using David to tell a sordid story about a seedy character rather than an inspirational story about a wonderful person who happens to be my son. David's story has now taken a turn for the worst, and I must press on with such unflattering details that I feel as though I'm verging on the point of being tasteless.

Truth of the matter is, David's life spawns travesties. I just happen to write. I strive to write well no matter what the topic is. David wanted me to write his story. To do an exceptional job on behalf of my son would be a thrill. In order to tell his story effectively, I have to get into the unpleasant details. Ours is not the most perfect or beautiful of collaborations, but it's the best we can do under the circumstances. Writing David's story, is essentially, reliving his story. His life consumes me. His excessive needs took my imagination hostage almost two decades ago. I'm on a quest to reclaim my imagination, and this is one of the books I must write before I can move on.

After David's arrest, he spent the weekend in jail. The following Monday, the court permitted Gena and me to take him home on a condition that is called "third-party custodian" in the state of Alaska. This was a get-out-of-jail pass with one condition: David must remain in our sight or within speaking distance of us for twenty-four hours a day, seven days a week, in what would transpire as the not-so-speedy processing of his case. Gena and I volunteered to watch David because we love him, and because the only other option was to let him remain in jail for an undeterminable amount of time.

Since David is under the third-party custodian requirement, he had to give up his apartment. Gena and I spent the weekend cleaning up the nightmare of his trashed accommodations. He's now camped in what used to be my office. To reach my desk the other night to grab my dictionary, I had to scale a mountain of video gamer paraphernalia, lunge across a double bed, and traverse several piles of dirty clothes. Try and tell a grown man to clean his room (even though it's your office) and you don't get too far. Right now I'm sitting on the couch with my feet propped up on the coffee table with a laptop burning a hole into my thighs.

I'm stressed to the point of sleeplessness most nights. I count restful moments these days in minutes of grateful unconsciousness or in sublime daydreams where I imagine what life could have been. I feel as if I am folding inward on myself like an origami figurine—beautifully composed on the outside, twisted and deformed on the inside. The injustices in David's life have been mounting since his accident, multiplying in frequency and intensity up to the

Picking Wings Off Butterflies

point of this latest fiasco. I wish to find a reason for the madness that has become our lives, but I can peer no further than beyond the fog of chaos. These past months will surely shave a few years off my life—and Gena's life—of this I'm certain.

Just days ago the most depressing realization entered my mind. I'd given it some thought before, but it didn't really sink in until this pivotal moment. Simply put, I have been taking care of David for twenty-six years, and I will in some way be taking care of David for the REST OF MY LIFE! And I don't want to do it anymore. The frustrating part? I don't have a choice.

Like most parents, I looked forward to my son becoming an adult, moving out of the house, and doing great things. I also understood that, before my son moved out, we'd share many difficult yet wonderful experiences. Initially, there would be endless months of waking to his cries and having to warm baby bottles during sleepless nights to make sure he survived his first year. There would be his toddler years when he was bound to crack his head on the corner of a table while learning how to walk or split his chin on concrete when he fell learning how to run. The elementary years would then follow with countless trips to emergency rooms for other mishaps. When he got to high school, I'd have to vicariously experience with him adolescence and puberty. There might be a battle with alcohol or experimental drugs I'd have to help him win. Perhaps he might even get a girl pregnant. When he earned his driver's license, his mother and I would spend anxious nights hoping he hadn't gotten into a head-on collision. After he graduated from high school, I'd take him to lunch and educate him on a course of study he should consider for college. Maybe I'd advise him not to get a liberal arts degree. I might even steer him away from writing or music as a vocation—that is, if he wanted to put food on his table. And I'd look forward to the awkward dinner when he brought a nice girl home for us to meet, then subsequently got married and fathered grandkids for me to spoil. All this would be done by the time he was, well... about as old as he is now. Then I'd be done. I would have been thinking, *WOW! That was exhausting but great! We had some tough times, but it was all worth it. I'm so proud of that boy! Now he's got his whole life ahead of him, and just look at where he's going next.* But that is not going to happen—EVER!

I'm wondering, am I selfish? Yeah, a little. Aren't we all? But am I human? Meaning, can I forgive myself for being selfish, for being rightfully upset that my life's not going to pan out the way I imagined it to?

Because I would really love to spend what little time I have left on earth doing what I want to do. What I love to do is write, and while I haven't felt much like writing for months, the art still brings me immense pleasure. This process is, at the moment, synonymous with scrolling back into my memories of David's life and finding a purpose to his existence in a way that might enrich others. And while his arrest might have blindsided me and knocked me off my pace, I will endeavor now to move on and continue with his story.

CHAPTER 10

A SEX CHANGE

*W*hen David started walking again, he gave us no indication he'd like to be walking in high heels as a woman some day. That shocking conversation would take place years later. In fact, David was nothing but boy once he hit the ground running in San Antonio. He was back to his old tricks, like terrorizing his little sister, which is just what any parent should expect from a rambunctious son.

Dana had an entire zoo of stuffed animals meticulously placed around her room. Many of them were lounging at the head of her bed as though ready to escort her to dreamland, and a half dozen or so were huddled together in the corner next to her dresser. Even the tiniest fluff balls received preferential treatment and were selected to inhabit choice spots on her nightstand. She was so conscientious in the placement of her furry friends that it bugged me. Children shouldn't be this fanatical about making sure everything in life is perfectly structured. It's downright unhealthy. So, every once in a while, I'd slip into her room and displace one of the creatures by an inch or so. Then I'd ask her, "Dana, how come your animals aren't where they should be?" This sent her world into a tizzy until she found the animal that was not exactly where she'd left it.

For a short period of time, Dana even got into the habit of sleeping on top of her bedspread. She said the reason she slept this way was so that she didn't have to mess up her bed and make it every morning. I fixed her of this obsession pronto by messing up her bed every time she didn't get under the covers and mess it up herself.

Anyway, David got a kick out of moving her animals too. Sometimes he'd grab Eli the elephant and toss him against a wall, or send Lacy the lamb bouncing down the hallway. Dana would let out this horrendous scream, since she was certain all her stuffed animals had feelings and could experience pain! When her Barbie doll disappeared, we suspected David was the culprit. Months passed before we found her doll's head under a bush in the front yard, and her torso near the backyard fence.

David was also dismembering his GI Joes, incinerating his toy cars, experimenting with superglue, pissing all over the toilet, and doing a thousand other things little boys do. One day at a fast-food restaurant, we got out of the car and David promptly urinated in the parking lot halfway to the front door. He just stopped mid-street, pulled it out, and was done before we saw the small river flowing. He'd picked up the habit of pissing in public in Europe—although Europeans are much more discreet about it—where public bathrooms can be really tough to locate.

There's a photograph in one of our photo albums that shows Dana and David sitting next to each other in our living room. Dana's the one bawling in the photo, and

Picking Wings Off Butterflies

David's smirking. He'd pinched her—again. Not in a mean way, but like someone might pinch a cute puppy. One day, the kids discovered talcum powder and Vaseline. Combine these two ingredients and they form a velvety, cement-like compound. We had to chase the greasy little Caspers down the hallway and right into the shower. Another day, they pulled the water hose out to a dry patch of dirt underneath the huckleberry tree in our backyard. They flooded the area and made their own kind of bath. There was nothing we could do but grab the camera and join in the fun!

David and his sister Dana, San Antonio, Texas, 1991

All this innocent terrorizing and getting into trouble on David's part suited me fine. David being a pain in the butt was exactly what I wanted him to be at that age. It beat the alternatives. He could've still been in the hospital lying on his back in a coma or vegetating in front of the television in a wheelchair.

Not too long after regaining the ability to walk, David

also relearned how to ride a bike. Once he got rolling, he was out of sight and getting into even more trouble. When he started making friends in the neighborhood, he passed yet another milestone. His new friends could not have seen his brain injuries, but his physical handicaps were easily visible. The kids were accepting him the way he was despite his imperfections. This surprised me, because I expected David would have more trouble making and keeping friends. By strange coincidence, his frontal lobe damage actually helped him win over friends more easily, and I think it plays a large part in how likable David is today. This part of the brain helps control inhibitions, and David has had few inhibitions since the accident. He'll say just about anything, he is a comedian at heart, and he really sets people at ease with his easygoing temperament.

We enrolled him in karate, but he didn't enjoy the regimen enough to stick with the program. Later on, Gena and I tried to get him involved with any activity he showed an interest in, such as gymnastics, Scouts, and art classes. We bought a cheap aboveground pool that he could swim in to help increase the mobility of the muscles in his arms and legs. We'd been advised that children who played hard stood a better chance of warding off permanent brain damage and long-lasting physical handicaps. Play was top priority, but no activity or sport captivated his interest for more than a few weeks.

While David could walk, he sure wasn't graceful. His left femur was still pierced with screws and welded together with metal plates. For some reason, the plates bolted to his left thigh accelerated the growth of his left leg. He walked as if he was straddling the curb on the street. Also, from the time David relearned how to walk in San Antonio, he had been walking on his tiptoes. To this day, he never uses his heels unless standing. Walking on tiptoes without special shoes is difficult enough for ballerinas to do for a few hours. David chose to do this indefinitely. Between two different-size legs and walking on his tiptoes, it's not difficult to imagine that people probably thought we started him out in the morning by pouring whiskey on his cornflakes instead of milk.

Then there is the issue of David's left upper extremity. He's practically forgotten he has a left arm and hand to use. More likely, his brain was not able to reroute itself to make them work properly, so most of the time his left arm just dangles by his side.

I'm partially paralyzed on my left side. I forget to use my left arm. This hasn't been cured yet. I don't believe it will. I've been told that if I use it I would strengthen it. It's not the fact that I don't want to use it. It's that it doesn't occur to me that it's there. My dad is the one person who would always tell me you have a left arm, David. He even bought me a drum set to help strengthen it and to find me something to do, but with my ADHD and lack of attention span I was never able to fully get into it.

David was attending speech therapy primarily to help him articulate words and regain expression in his voice. He also spoke in monotone with little or no tonal variation to his vocalizations. It's a curiosity how language works. One has to speak in a certain way and with clarity in order for people to understand. Speak in garbled expressions and you might as well be speaking in a foreign language. We had to relearn how to interpret much of what David was saying. As the years progressed, he became more articulate and we understood him better.

Well, now that I'm aware of what happened, and have rejoined the ability to walk and talk, I'm learning that the medical community is not through with me—not even close. Dana and Grandma are here [San Antonio] and the next thing I remember (if I'm remembering correctly) is appointments, appointments, appointments, appointments. We have to find out what I'm capable of and what are my flaws; what are my neurological problems. Then again, we are still in the moving process and here it is, our new home. I don't recall living in a house until age seven. It was a one-story brown brick/wood house on a street called Village Glen. To our left is Brenda's house, one of my sister's closest friends. Dad goes back to Germany to finish out his time in the service and I begin my time in school. Fun. Fun.

I had to be put in special education classes. I remember riding the bus with kids in my class. One whose name I don't remember, always carried with him a plastic toy cow. I also remember going to PE (Physical Education) and having to sit out while the class was going on because of my disabilities. I also wet my pants at school several times on account of laughter. Summer vacations seemed like forever back then. I mean they were long and fun. My mother or grandmother would take us to McDonald's quite often it seems and let us play in the park.

I was finally coming around to being semi-normal, although once I know I have a problem I'm well aware of it, and keep tabs on what I can do and how I do it, although my methods of doing something differ from your normal, average Joe. This was another reason I would get into trouble and it has kept up with me till today. It took some time for me to realize that it's a struggle for me to grasp how to do something and succeed in doing it, and I think this learning disability is what stood in my way as a child and quite frequently is a problem that gets on my nerves.

Picking Wings Off Butterflies

After the accident it became clear to me rather quickly that I wasn't like other children anymore. I soon realized that I was the exception to average Joe and that being said, I would have more trouble than most kids my age. Like other kids I would have problems to deal with, but unlike other kids I would have a bit more difficulty dealing with my problems and with my disabilities. I would have a much harder time being accepted by children and adults. I began to realize at an early age that people in general look down on people with disabilities, and that's always been a problem.

I've always felt I had to compete to win people over, and this really began to give me grief as I got older, but for now I was young and with a feeling of loneliness. Even though I made friends and participated in play or activities, I've been under the impression that I'm the parasite. I don't think that any of my childhood friends at the time I was in elementary school really accepted me. I was a parasite to them, and any further contact with me seems like it would contaminate them, so I suppose out of fear they were hesitant in being my friend.

I read into these thoughts David expresses that even at an early age he was having a difficult time fitting in. And what I learned as he later passed through middle school and even beyond high school was that in his desperation to have a normal life he would do just about anything for anybody. It's typical, of course, for people to tweak their personalities or interests a bit in order to maintain friendships, but David can morph his character beyond recognition at times. Sure, he's got certain traits that are quintessentially David. But what he had not developed—even by the time he had entered his twenties—was a basic concept of who he really was. Which explains in part why he so nonchalantly told me one day in Alaska that he wanted to have a sex change.

You see, David doesn't have normal, run-of-the-mill problems. David has life-changing physical and psychological issues that require us to suspend our lives until these issues get resolved. Here's just a few examples I can offer that have transpired throughout the course of his life: There was the time David thought he had colon cancer. There are the dozens of heart attack scares he's had throughout his life. There was the time an officer at our front door informed us David was involved in a fender bender hit-and-run. There was another time we found out David actually had two fender bender hit-and-runs. There was the other accident in which he practically collapsed our garage by knocking out the center beam with the car. There was the night he totaled the truck Gena bought me for Christmas, an accident that nearly killed him. There are the times he hears voices and thinks he is a schizophrenic. There was the time he was going to marry a high school sweetheart and we had to talk him out of it. There were his drug years, (which I'll get into shortly). There were the times I had to dash to the courthouse to pay for his traffic tickets. There was the time he got arrested. There were the three times we spent getting him registered for college then he promptly quit. There were the innumerable job training programs we helped set up for him, which he also quit. There were the half dozen times we packed his bags and drove him to inpatient care facilities to be treated. There was the time he missed his high school graduation, because he went into a drug stupor and we found him thirty miles down south at the house of yet another girl whom he was determined to marry. There was another officer who rang the doorbell and wanted to question David about a robbery in a hotel room. There was the time he called us at ten o'clock at night from a pay phone a three-hour drive north of Austin and needed a ride home. There was the other

Picking Wings Off Butterflies

time we had to talk him out of marrying a third fiancée and moving to Washington State. There was the time he set fire to his room. There was the time he traded his moped for a tattoo and we finally bought him a pedal bike. And there were a hundred other events—events similar to these but seem too trivial for me to even write down, much less elaborate on—that would otherwise qualify as crises when compared to the bad things normal kids do.

Phew! Anyway...

One Friday afternoon David informed me that he wanted to be a woman. He didn't need a few bucks to pay the light bill, didn't need advice on which job to take, he only wanted to be a woman. Simple. I had just picked him up from his apartment, because he was going to spend the weekend with us. While in the truck on the drive home, he started rambling an odd and vague confession. I'm not much of a talker when I drive, and I err on the side of safety. I usually see one or two ginormous moose on the stretch between our house and town. It has been said that moose make a big impression when you hit them, and I'd prefer not to totally crush the front end of my truck. From what David's flapping on about, it seems to me that a few of his misguided friends have convinced him that something's askew with his behavior.

I'll confess, I'm becoming much more insensitive to David's issues as the years progress. The vast accumulation of David's ills and woes has resulted in a rather cold and automated response on my part: I tend to brush his problems aside as though they were snowflakes on my jacket.

Think of it this way. When calamities are the norm in one's life, then calamities will drive a person crazy if one doesn't minimize their relevance. One learns to set a certain emotional value to the events that transpire in one's life, and taking care of an individual with special needs raises the bar of what constitutes a truly horrific emergency. An event that some individuals might rate as a level nine emergency and that might happen once in a person's lifetime would be a level two occurrence for me. The reason I downscale their relevance is because I likely went through a similar situation last month, which was quite similar to the emergency I dealt with last year.

I call this aptitude to minimize one's emotional threshold a *calamity disassociation disorder*. You may use the acronym CDD. I question whether I'm hopelessly insensitive. Surely, there are other men in my predicament. As men, we have to be tough. Our culture expects it. If I seem insensitive to David's problems, it's because—man to man—I have an obligation to toughen David up as well. That's what I tell myself. Anyway, I could take medication for my CDD, except the pills haven't been concocted in a lab yet. But even if they were invented, I wouldn't take them anyway out of fear I'd become impotent or have a stroke or get cancer, all of which are common side effects of many prescription medications peddled by the pharmaceutical industry these days. Ironically, marijuana is still a crime in most states, and it's most noticeable side effect is giving people an acute case of the munchies. Go figure.

"What's that, David? Did you say something? Your friends think you've been out of sorts lately?"

He stumbled for the right words as though lost in a daydream. "Well, it's kind of like I'm a different person. They see a different person in me popping in and out from time to time."

I was thinking schizophrenia. I negotiated a few more turns, searching for moose and bears.

"Everybody wants to be somebody else from time to time," I told him.

I'm pretty sure David isn't a schizophrenic. He has never exhibited any of the signs of having multiple personalities. But I was way off target anyway. While David was hinting at being two people in one, he was hoping I'd confess that I had always thought he was more girl than boy.

He finally gathered the courage to express himself. "My friends think I act like a woman more than I act like a man."

"Well, David, in a way, people are both male and female. Sometimes males act more female, but they are still very much male. And it's not uncommon to imagine or wonder what it might be like to be a woman. Maybe you're just recognizing these female qualities in you."

I was trying my best to alleviate his concerns that he had two people wandering through his mind, one named David and the other named, possibly, Delilah. But my five-cent opinion didn't satisfy him.

Moments later, we pulled up to the house without a new furry grille ornament. Ten minutes later, Gena and I were engaged in a battle of words to convince David he wasn't a woman. The crisis began in the truck and escalated into an hour-long "discussion" at the kitchen table, at which point I was rendered speechless and mumbled my way out the back door to the log pile with him in hot pursuit.

I began splitting my frustration into kindling. At one point, I threw a joke his way to break the tension. I can't remember exactly what I said, but I asked him something like, "Why don't you have normal problems, David? I would just be thrilled to death if the issue you had this weekend was that you had gotten a girl pregnant or you'd joined the marines to serve your country and were headed to Iraq. Why does our family time this weekend have to center around us trying to convince you that you're not a woman?"

When it comes to David's fleeting interests, they have a tendency to evaporate in a few days like puddles of muck in a parched desert. What is often the case, though, is that he becomes entirely fixated on his ideas until they possess his mind and take over every waking moment of our lives. For Gena and me, this means we must deal with David's passing issues on a perpetual basis, where one crisis passes and is immediately succeeded by another crisis, and most are unresolvable anyway, because they were concocted in his mind and have no basis in reality.

David didn't want to be a woman. I knew it and Gena knew it. A week later, David was embarrassed to admit he even considered the notion. David was intrigued by the idea of undergoing a complete transformation of his life, which is something we all think about from time to time.

CHAPTER 11

FIRES ON THE HOME FRONT

Having been in the army, I'd earned the right to a veteran's loan, and I was ready to cash in on the benefit. We bought our first home in northwest San Antonio for a hundred dollars down. Although the down payment was paltry, it about killed me to write the check. The reason being, Gena and I had gotten so used to moving around that once I signed the contract, I thought our adventuresome days would be over.

The army had done its best to coax me to reenlist, but there were plenty of reasons to pass up the offer. The personnel department still had not gotten my missing pay reconciled, which placed an unnecessarily stressful financial burden on us. The way the army handled David's transfer out of Frankfurt and subsequent medical care, which for me did not seem to be as aggressive as it should have been, had me considering the benefits of looking into the public health care system. Then there was the issue of how the army had me gallivanting back across the Atlantic to sit at a desk in Frankfurt while my family desperately needed my help stateside. These factors and others made my decision not to reenlist a no-brainer.

My recruiter had told me upon enlisting that my training as a tactical satellite systems operator should land me a great job as a civilian in the rapidly growing telecommunications field. He didn't promise anything; I just mistook the word *should* for *would*. After months of sending out resumes, I learned there were no jobs in the field I'd trained in. So I did what came naturally, I opened a landscaping and lawn business. This was the kind of work I had always enjoyed doing, and I liked the idea of working for myself and taking off whenever I wanted to go on a vacation. As an added incentive, we got to have the nicest lawn in our new neighborhood. I was able to obtain most of the plants in my yard wholesale, and I had extra help from my employees in providing the labor to make the place look as nice as it could. But were it not for my impromptu firefighting skills, our lovely home on the block would not be standing there today.

"Hey," David said to me nonchalantly one evening. "I set my curtains on fire."

He was talking in his monotone drone like he was reading from a book, which didn't even warrant me taking my eyes off my own book.

"What do you mean your curtains are on fire?" I asked without looking at him.

"I was playing with a lighter on the windowsill and the curtains caught fire."

Now he was getting into details. Reality set in, and I went flying upstairs, through the game room, down the hall, and into his room. Sure enough, his curtains had been

Picking Wings Off Butterflies

transformed into huge tiki torches! The popcorn ceiling above them was melting and peeling off! Noxious black smoke was filling the room!

One can never move too elegantly in an emergency of this magnitude. I ripped the curtains off their rods and threw them on the floor. I grabbed the pillow off the bed to smother the curtains. Then the carpet and the pillow caught fire. While reaching for a blanket to smother the carpet, I inadvertently threw the pillow on the bed. Then the bed ignited. I stood for a moment dumbfounded that the bed was erupting into flames, and when I looked down, the carpet had set the blanket ablaze. It is truly amazing how fast carpet, pillows, blankets, and mattresses burn. I'd swear they are all manufactured out of flammable foam soaked in jet fuel. The next few minutes were a whirl of flailing arms and dancing feet as I grabbed more blankets to suffocate the flames and threw cups of water on the last remaining puffs of smoke.

When we moved into the house, David was entering the third grade. Due to his accident, he'd fallen behind a year. Academically he was doing okay, but it was hard to tell at this stage in his life, because during the early years of elementary school all children seem to be functioning at a similar level. Reading, for example, is rudimentary in grade school, and the same holds true for simple mathematics. Practically every child in the third grade can add two plus two and read, "See Spot Run." But in retrospect, long division and word problems were beginning to be particularly difficult for David.

These days, now an adult, David still has difficulty understanding proverbial sayings. Sayings like "Better to kill two birds with one stone," "Time is on our side," and "Don't count your chickens before they hatch" have him scratching his head. Same goes with riddles, which are just clever word problems except without the math. What David always understands are jokes. "Did you hear about the blonde who . . . ?" "Why did the chicken cross the road?" David can wrap his mind around any set of words that makes him laugh.

David says his best subject was spelling followed by social studies. This computes. Right now I have David reading through the first draft of his story as I complete each chapter. I want to make sure I'm getting the details correct. I also want him to feel comfortable with what we are choosing to reveal. All he has to do is say the word and I'll snip out of its pages any unflattering tale or detail he's not comfortable with including.

After he finished reading a chapter one day, he approached me at the kitchen table and said, "You misspelled a word."

"I don't doubt it," I replied.

"Here in chapter two you wrote *barely* when you should have written *rarely*."

"Technically, that's not a misspelled word," I told him. "I mistakenly typed a *b* and the spell-checker didn't catch the error." I felt vindicated but also proud that he'd caught the mistake.

Another thing I tend to do is mumble or speak in my own words. I mean, I say things for no reason, and the things I say make no sense. Not to worry though. I don't have Tourette Syndrome.

I've gotten used to David's mumbling at imaginary friends and his cussing at his video game characters when they don't do what his fingers and thumbs are frantically

Picking Wings Off Butterflies

trying to make them do. He still holds regular conversations with himself, usually when he's alone, but it's still distressing for me. I feel like I should interrupt him and offer him a real person to converse with. We've all been known to say things out loud to ourselves. Perhaps with David his thoughts just spill out more regularly than they normally would, because the proper mental barricades are not in place.

More distressing is the fact that Gena and I can't have intelligent discussions with our son. He mumbles in tones similar to baby talk at times, he says things for no reason, and he says things that make no sense. Much of this has to do with David's overall intelligence level and his childlike interests. Gena and I think he's about six to eight years behind the curve. There are times when he says things that mimic what a student in high school might say. Then there are times when he acts his present age.

What primarily occupies David's time these days are video games and a select genre of fighting and horror movies. If he watches television, he watches animated cartoon shows. I have nothing against playing video games and watching these kinds of shows. What I will say is that since David's mind is filled with the images, vocabulary, and overall ideals espoused by these shows, this limits the age and intelligence level of the people he can hold conversations with.

I think playing video games and watching television about six hours a day has also affected David's ability to concentrate on anything for more than a few minutes at a time. It's likely his life races along in micro-moments, and when reality does intrude, he treats these intrusions as though they were commercial breaks in his favored stream of consciousness. He never quite absorbs what's going on in the present moment, and he seems to be mentally acting on the premise that life is about to flip to a different channel or—similar to a video game—advance to a different level at any given moment. Sometimes, when he appears most confused in the present moment, it seems as though he's "rebooting" or "returning to start," without having fully grasped what just transpired. Then again, the way he thinks may not be a result of his brain injuries after all, but rather it's indicative of how we are all trying to process and cope with the mountains of informational bits that dazzle our senses in an increasingly complex, technological landscape. Who has time these days to go and sit for thirty minutes and become immersed in the spiritual experience of watching a setting sun when it's more easy to populate the pixels of a computer screen with a similar image with just the click of a mouse? We are all becoming quite accustomed to pseudo-stimulation and techno-gratification.

By far, the issue that prevents his mother and me from really engaging with our son is his inability to focus on the present moment. Indeed, David seems to retain less than half of what he's experiencing. I'd estimate that David recalls less than 20 percent of our conversations with him. We are often having the same conversations over and over and over again. Consequently, while I'd love to chat with my son at any time, my dialogues with David must remain few and brief. When I speak to him, I must first recognize that while he's looking directly at me, he will likely remember little I say to him. I must also keep my words simple and on target in order for him to maximize the expressions he might remember. Factor in David's nonsensical comments and his mumbling, and conversing with David becomes more of a task than a pleasure.

But occasionally, during rare moments, David will surprise me with deep thoughts and express philosophical and even metaphysical challenges. When he has these insights, he reveals to me that he's still engaged in the enchanting world of human thought. Somewhere in that brain of his, the original David is lurking. I know he's in there. Now, if I could just coax him to come out more often.

When we were growing up in Germany before the accident, the only person I really had to play with was my sister. We had some good times. After the accident I think we drifted. I mean, we still talk and all, but we don't kick it like we used to. She was the one person though who really understood me and still does, probably more than I do myself.

Dana is two years younger than David. They've been close since the accident. I hesitate to compare her with David, except to say she's normal. What I mean by *normal* is that she represents what we expected to experience as parents when raising our daughter. More to the point, she gave us little grief while growing up, and it has been delightful to watch her mature into a young woman. From day one, Dana fostered a sensitivity toward David's predicament, which she exhibits to this day. Though younger, she has been David's big sister, often sticking up for him in school and social gatherings. She could have ostracized David—she would have been more popular if she had—but she made the point of including David in her life.

While growing up, Dana was a model child. Her natural goodness was cultivated by her appreciation of the difficulties brought into our family's life by David's accident. In other words, she could have been a real teenage nightmare of a girl, but when she recognized how much difficulty David and her parents were having, she spared us the headache of acting up herself. She could have gotten into drugs, gotten pregnant, joined a cult, and otherwise made us sick with worry, but she didn't do any of these things. I actually recall only one evening when she broke curfew, and I had to drive into town and round her up—seriously, one time.

So by middle school I made myself out to be sort of a bad/shy kid and began to cause trouble. So much so, that I had to be removed from a Christian church school and put in public school. I think by that time I was beginning to get restless about not being able to fit in. I began to present myself differently and began to delve into using profane language as part of my English, but was still conscious that I had to watch out, because there's always someone bigger and tougher than me. While portraying a tough kid I was still timid and tried to avoid confrontation.

Our family had been attending a Seventh-day Adventist church on the northwest side of San Antonio. The church offered a private school, and we thought the experience would be good for David. We were beginning to recognize the inadequacies of the public school system in educating children with handicaps and learning disabilities. We thought a smaller student-to-teacher ratio would provide David with targeted instruction and help him develop better social skills. We were informed just a few months later that David was a "discipline" problem. The teacher could no longer teach her regular students, because she was devoting so much time to educating David. I wondered at the time, *If David has learning disabilities that require more hands-on instruction from the teacher, how does this qualify him as being a discipline problem?* But I suppose he could have been considered unruly, given America's cookie-cutter and rigid approach to education. Anyway, we promptly reenrolled David in the public system.

Picking Wings Off Butterflies

Four years later, after moving into our first home, Gena was offered a job as the patient care manager for a hospice in Austin, Texas. The promotion would be a sizable step up for her and an opportunity we couldn't pass up. My landscaping business was in full swing, but I could easily start anew in Austin. All I had to do was hook up my trailer full of equipment and go. We rented a house in Austin and promptly moved.

As a couple, Gena and I drifted apart shortly after our move to Austin. In hindsight, we'd begun separating emotionally years earlier. In no way was David responsible for our soon-to-come physical separation, but I'd be lying if I quipped that the stresses of taking care of a special needs child don't affect the relationship that parents have to each other—because these stresses can be pivotal. Gena and I really have only ourselves to blame for what we did not do to keep our love alive. As for not keeping my family together, the fault was all mine, because after Gena and I separated, I got on a plane and traveled to the other side of the world.

During this time we began to move. My dad was in Korea now teaching English and my mom was with me and my sister.

Why I considered teaching English in Korea to escape my troubles at home is a mystery now shrouded in faulty memories of stupid excuses that no longer can be rationalized. People do dimwitted things at highly stressful times and when confronted with hard choices. We are often overwhelmed with a barrage of conflicting emotions and ideas, which makes it seem like we have few choices. I suppose that's why the absurd and ridiculous choices begin to appear sensible. In the chaos of confused thought, we can't see through the fog to pick the best course of action to solve our troubles. Mistakes will happen. Bad choices will be made. These are my excuses.

This was an extremely frustrating time for me compounded by my inability to restart my business in Austin and make a decent living. Before I packed my bags, I spent many evenings outside on the porch thinking through my options. There were plenty of local jobs I could have taken, but I was not looking for a real job. I was looking for an adventure that would take me away from the reality of what had become my life. I saw an ad seeking English teachers overseas, I applied for a position, and then I signed a twelve-month contract. Weeks later, I was flying all the way to Iksan, South Korea.

The feelings I had upon arriving in Korea were similar to the emotions I went through when I arrived in Frankfurt. While in the army, my first post was located in an ancient four-story German army barrack left over from WWII. After checking in to my unit on the ground floor, I climbed the old building's winding staircase up to the attic. The attic was filled with rows of bunkbeds and clothes lockers, and it doubled as temporary housing for the soldiers processing in and out of the unit. Rain pelted the dinky dormer windows along the room. As I peered outside, I thought of my family thousands of miles away. I distinctly remember asking myself, *How the hell did you end up here?*

Similarly, I arrived in South Korea just after sunset. My hosts took me to dinner, and I burned my hand on a superheated stone bowl of *talsot bibimpap*. It's a dish made of layers of rice, mixed vegetables, meat and topped with a fried egg. The ingredients need to be aggressively stirred, and I made the mistake of grabbing the bowl to keep the contents from pouring over the edges. I was then dropped off at my new apartment, which sat above a home owned by a family

Picking Wings Off Butterflies

that was in the auto parts business. My host and I climbed up the skinny cement staircase about and foot and a half wide to the roof. A tin porch of sorts surrounded my tiny apartment, and the space under the porch held steel racks stuffed with chrome bumpers, unpainted doors, and other kinds of car parts. Later that evening, while looking over the walls of the yard surrounding my apartment, I gazed at the sprawling layers of ancient homes and modern buildings in the distance and thought, *What the hell are you doing here?*

My wife and I were now officially separated. At first—I dare say—we were enjoying some much-needed time away from each other. After all, I'd proposed to Gena in college in Texas when she was seventeen and I was twenty. We were barely out of kid-hood. When we married a year later in Arizona, I had the sum total of twenty-five cents in the pocket of my rented tux. No kidding. What I did have was an overabundance of faith—or just a naive presumption—and this paid well. The minister who married us returned the $50.00 payment we offered him to perform our wedding services. A local doctor in the church gave us a gift of $200.00. There were a few other envelopes at the wedding ceremony that also contained cash. These cash gifts were godsends, giving us just enough money to buy gas and foodstuffs to get us back to Texas, where we were attending college. The official honeymoon would have to wait—and it still waits.

I mention this bit of history to say that neither one of us had much time to enjoy life as individuals after we met each other. Once we married, David and Dana arrived on the scene rather quickly, and we still had a few years to go before finishing college. After college, we ran headlong into life, and just a few short years later, we were in Frankfurt. Then David had his accident, and we have been dealing with the challenges that this misfortune has caused ever since.

At the end of my first year in Korea, I promptly signed up for another tour. I obtained a better teaching position the second time around with Wonkwang University, instructing in its English as a Second Language (ESL) program. While waiting for my second contract to begin, I returned home for a few months to visit, and Gena was kind enough to let me stay at her house.

The night I left for Korea again, I was running late. Gena and Dana were giving me a ride to the airport. We rushed into an IHOP restaurant and wolfed down our dinner. Whomever invented the word *good-bye* was an idiot; a complete moron. There is no such thing as a good goodbye. Gena knew I was leaving, and she had time to mentally adjust to my running away again. For my daughter, it must have seemed like she went out with Daddy to eat pancakes one night and he disappeared for another year. To this day, I get sick to my stomach regurgitating the memory.

CHAPTER 12

"DISABLED PEOPLE THINK DIFFERENT"

I get mad real easily. I tend to stay mad for a while, but usually can calm myself down rather quickly. With me, when I get upset, I tend to obsess on it or keep it going with an argument. I don't like to be the person who is wrong.

"No one likes to be wrong, David."

During my first year in Korea, Gena and I talked by phone and wrote letters to each other about work and the kids, but not about us. I was still mad, and I wasn't ready to admit that she had a right to be mad either. My grasp of our situation was that we were merely taking a short reprieve from each other. I was no doubt presumptuous—or cognitively impaired. During the early months of my second year in Korea, we divorced. We talked even less after our divorce for about six months, during which time we both enjoyed the freedom of being unhitched. Yet, after these months passed, we both realized we'd made a big mistake in letting each other go. I came to realize that if I didn't return from gallivanting around Korea, I'd lose her forever, and possibly rarely see my children.

I'm not proud of deserting my wife and family. (At least this is the excuse I use to beat myself up with when I think about this escapade in our lives.) And this memory is like poison—a shock to my soul that pops into my consciousness without warning from time to time and steals my breath away. There's no antidote for this poison. Only the passing of time slowly evaporates some of the pain, but a tinge of it always remains.

As much as Gena and I may have wronged each other, and considering the things I said and did that led to our separation, the thought that plagued me the most was my desire to run from the responsibilities of raising David. When I initially got on that plane to Korea, leaving David was not a conscious desire. Now that I've gained the benefit of perspective, I realize I did disappear in part to get a break from David. But I don't entirely regret my actions. Ultimately, I want to be free from David. I want to live a life independent of his incessant needs. I also want David to live his own life free of his parents' guardianship.

It's been said that the perfect father is one who makes sacrifices to ensure that his children enjoy a better life than his own. My perspective is somewhat different. What's been said is an idealistic notion easily spoken but a platitude nevertheless. We all have a mental threshold and a pressure-release valve that limits the amount of emotional trauma we can contain within ourselves. When the physical and emotional traumas in life build up and become too much for our brains to handle, we must find a way to release that pressure. At times, this means that we personally have to find a way to escape the environment. And let's face it, life can be tough. Most of us have the fortitude to overcome the obstacles we will encounter, but few can take on the emotional stress of another person's life on top of their own, even when that other person is their child, and especially when that child has special needs. To borrow a truism: life is a game of surviving—whether it be emotional or physical survival—we tend to fight or take flight. The natural course of action is to fight off both physical pain and emotional trauma until we are weakened to the point that taking flight becomes compulsory. When we take flight, we are removing ourselves from the situation that is causing us harm. And I think we do this for good reason: to gain strength to fight another day. I attribute this reaction as the true reason I first got on that plane bound for Korea.

Toward the end of my second-year contract for teaching in Korea, Gena bought a 1970s ranch-style home north of Austin. She sent me pictures of her new home surrounded by five acres of Texas hill country. Half the property was cleared and graced with tall grass, and the other half wooded with mature oak trees hanging over a meandering, muddy stream. Out back a large deck surrounded an aboveground pool. The landscaping needed a caretaker. The children playing in the pool needed a father. If only it were that easy to put myself back into the pictures of their lives.

Yet everything is as easy or as difficult as we imagine it to be. I was ready to forgive and forget with no conditions if Gena was ready to do likewise and have me back in her life. Anger can consume us like an out-of-control wildfire, and it rages on until the excuses we use to fuel the flames are exhausted. Only then, when the embers have cooled, can we somberly examine the charred remains of what has become our lives. Although getting over my anger took a couple of years, it was as if it cleared up overnight, like a southern storm that builds in the heat of the afternoon over troubled waters and dissipates in the cool of night. Sure, I could have continued fanning the flames and kept my anger red hot, but that would have guaranteed I'd forever remain estranged from the love of my life and the children we created.

The harder act of forgiveness would be for me to forgive David for something he ironically could not be blamed for, which was getting hit by that car.

Parents taking care of children with traumatic brain injuries or other handicaps discover in time that they must gingerly tiptoe through a quagmire of unique moral dilemmas. These moral challenges will also cause many to feel emotions such as anger, resentment, and guilt, just to name a few. To be truthful, I've been angry with David since the day he stepped foot onto that busy street. I've been angry with the woman who was driving the car that struck him. There is no logical reason for me to still be upset with David or the woman, I just am. I resent the years I've lost in which I have not been able to pursue my own life while taking care of David. My resentment serves no purpose, but it's a natural feeling I can't shake. And because I feel angry and resentful for seemingly no reason, I also feel guilty, because good fathers shouldn't have to feel these kinds of emotions or have these kinds of thoughts, right? Only the bad fathers do, because they're too busy feeding their own ego and wanting to live their own life. And this is the kind of vicious emotional cycle many parents will experience.

Since we cannot know the future, we cannot do anything to change the course of our own lives to circumvent tragedy, much less evade tragedy on behalf of our loved ones. Tragedies will come to all of us in varying degrees of severity. We can skew the odds of incurring a tragedy if we play it safe, hide out, and refuse to live. Likewise, we can keep our children from harm by overprotecting them, thus robbing them of a normal life, which would be a tragedy in its own right. When in the midst of tragedy, or perhaps after the fact, we will experience a wide range of unwelcome thoughts and emotions. These emotions are unavoidable. About the only choice we can make is not to be overcome by these emotions to the point that they destroy either our lives or the lives of those we love.

When I reflected on the metaphysical aspects of David's accident, I eventually concluded that he was merely a victim of an everyday occurrence, albeit a tragic event. In order for me to learn to live with this tragedy, I had to think through the logic of understanding that all human tragedies occur at random, and by virtue of their randomness, they are impartial events. Despite my religious upbringing, I had to conclude that no supernatural person or agency had set events in motion that led to David being struck by a car. More to the point, God did not place David at that precise street location at that preordained time. God was not to blame. Nor did I find a single tangible reason to believe that my own behavior had caused God to punish me personally by inflicting injury on my son or to teach anyone in my family a particular lesson. David merely crossed a busy street at the wrong time. And being able to suspend my previously held religious misconceptions about human tragedy and replace those beliefs with rational and realistic answers really went a long way toward silencing the emotional turmoil that had been plaguing my mind and pestering my soul.

Nevertheless, I find myself wagging my head at the absurdity of my reasoning, because my words only make sense to a person of reasonable intelligence. I mean, what happens when a brain injury or another kind of handicap prevents a person from understanding this chain of logic? Many individuals who experience life-altering events similar to David's will never be able to escape the idea that they have been singled out or that they are being punished by having to live a life few others are required to endure. You see, normal people have the capacity to rationalize and look at the bright side. They can at least find a way of making the best of the tragedy that has occurred in their lives. Most victims, especially those who suffer from serious head traumas, have likely lost much of the mental capacity to even rationalize effectively. They are victims twice over, because they will not be able to find a meaningful purpose to their lives, a purpose that makes sense anyway. Try as he may, David—and many in his situation—may never be able to intellectually grapple with understanding both the spiritual and factual implications of his predicament. You see, traditional spiritual beliefs tend to offer individuals comfort by permitting one to accept that the events of their lives are orchestrated with a divine purpose. In other words, they are taught to believe that whatever transpires in their lives is orchestrated for "good" reason. On the other hand, understanding tragedy from a purely rational perspective allows one to accept the simple laws of cause and effect—that is, that no spiritual implications need be applied to any event. And most assuredly, that tragic events are by no means to be construed as being "good." But understanding these spiritual nuances and challenging them with more rational explanations can be difficult or even impossible for those living with mental handicaps.

A distinction should be made, however, between people who have brain injuries and those who might otherwise be mentally or physically handicapped. Many physically handicapped individuals are easily recognized by their handicaps, and the intellectual deficits of those with mental handicaps are also often easily perceived. Consequently, people in general are willing to treat those individuals with the compassion they deserve. This is not necessarily true for individuals with traumatic brain injuries. TBI victims are born with a healthy mind. Post-injury, most have no discernible physical abnormalities, and their intellectual and emotional discrepancies cannot be seen. The result is that these individuals fall into the cracks of our society. They are made easy prey and are easily victimized. Many TBI victims are thought to be lazy and unintelligent—or worse, as individuals prone to deviant behavior. Few have the skills necessary to obtain an education or vocational training or to keep good jobs. Whereas there are special homes for the handicapped and psychiatric hospitals for the psychologically ill, there are few treatment facilities and specialized housing options for those with traumatic brain injuries.

David has written pages and pages of material for me to use in putting together his story. As I mentioned before, there are moments when his mind ponders deeper questions of his existence. From his notes I've gleaned these gems of thought that contain his own brand of philosophy. I don't necessarily agree with David's take on life, but that is irrelevant. What's important is that despite there being certain areas of David's brain that do not function quite like an average person's, David's mind is still engaged in finding his own way in this world.

You are only born once. Well, twice if you're religious (I am).

You cannot come into the world with your mind set on who you want to be and expect to be whatever you were thinking about.

Don't tell me everything's going to be all right. No it's not. Some problems never end.

Why ask why when the answer never brings up a real solution?

Expression=Opinion. Not everyone will care about what you think, but everyone will have an opinion about how you express yourself.

Maybe extinction means to let a life slip away to make more room for a better-equipped species.

When does an obsession become a lifestyle?

I don't like the death idea. As a matter of fact, I think it's very scary. I'm a Christian and I do believe in God, but since I've began to consider things I wonder often, why do we live when we are all going to die? To me that seems like a waste. What's the point of a beginning if it has to end? In my opinion, if you're going to start something don't stop. If you're going to make something, don't let it die.

And what happened in Eden a billion years ago should have stayed there. So, Eve fucked up. Let her go down for it. Not the entire human race. But I stick to my guns on religion. Even though in my opinion it's a little stricter than I'm normally comfortable with. But I stick it out for two reasons:

First, I believe in God. Second, I don't want to go to hell and burn for eternity.

Fear. Fear will drive people. It's motivation for everyone and more so for the people who live with conditions like mine.

Check this out. It is said in the Bible that people will be numbered as the sands of the earth. Everything on this earth has to do with numbers. I'm willing to bet that ideas alone outnumber humanity a billion to one.

Disabled people think different from people who don't have disabilities. I know. I've had more than my share of interaction with people who are disabled, and in my opinion the disabled in some instances think better than the average Joe.

Some people like me for who I am. Some people like me for what I could be.

In my experience life is about acceptance. If you don't have it, or what it takes to be accepted, you're just like bubbles floating in the wind.

CHAPTER 13

Separation Anxiety

If you are ever returning home from South Korea and flying from Kunsan to Seoul, you may witness the airport employees offering a symbolic gesture of gratitude for your stay. From the baggage boys to the clerks at the ticket counter, from the food vendors who restock the galleys to the guys refueling the planes, all the employees rush out of the building, head out to the tarmac, and line up shoulder to shoulder. You'll wonder what they're doing as they frantically grip their hats and bobble about in the wind gusts as the turbines from the engines start to whine. Then you watch as they bow—not a flippant bow—but a slow and deliberate bow signifying a measure of respect to their departing guests.

Koreans also offer a high level of respect to their teachers, known as *seonsaengnims*. I was a foreign teacher, but their respect for me would have been no different had I been one of their own instructors. It was a pleasure to have inhabited

Picking Wings Off Butterflies

this realm in their culture. Korea now seems like a dream, but if I think hard enough, the memories return.

My students were forever taking me out to eat. They fed me extremely well, and I rarely paid the tab. My students thought nothing of picking me up unannounced at any time and driving me hours to a remote mountain or seaside restaurant where we feasted on freshly fried octopus, raw fish lettuce wraps, Korean-marinated barbecue, and many other exotic dishes. We usually washed down our food with *soju*, which is a twenty- or twenty-five-proof clear liquor that will smooth the rough edges off any bilingual conversation.

Evenings on the weekends often ended in a *norebong* (a singing room) after dinner. No excuses, everyone sings in Korea. Most *norebongs* also served food and *soju*, so even if you didn't feel inclined to sing initially, your inhibitions were eventually subdued. Some weekends I went to a *videobong*, where I could rent a video and watch it in one of the booths while seated on a comfortable couch. English-speaking movies were subtitled using Hangul, the remarkably easy-to-read and write Korean alphabet. If I picked out a Korean movie, I usually couldn't understand much of what the actors were saying, but it's amazing how much of a language and culture can be understood through context and body language.

I bought a used car, a Hyundai Sonata, and traveled around the country as much as I dared. The roads are skinny, and the traffic signs use European symbols with words written in Hangul. The traffic cops wear white pants held up by a shiny white belt. They also wear bright blue shirts. Most of the officers don't carry guns, but they still strap the white gun holsters onto their belts. Then they stand off to the side of the road and practically jump out in front of your car if they catch you breaking a traffic rule. To get you to stop, they'll flag you down with an orange wand, and if you fail to yield, they'll yell into a walkie-talkie to tell the officer down the road (the one with the gun) to stop you. My students told me that some officers might flag me over just to get pocket money. I was forced to a screeching halt on three separate occasions. The officers looked baffled every time they pulled me over and appeared genuinely upset when they couldn't communicate with me. Funny how I forgot all the Hangul I learned while they stood there yelling at me! But hey, I was nervous and never did get a ticket.

You will need a fan for sleeping at night in the summer. Prop it up next to your bed so it blows on you all night long. Every once in a while, the mosquito truck will roll down the street, sending ascending poisonous gases up and over nearby apartment buildings. You'll want to close your window to prevent choking to death. The water's probably okay, but boil and stockpile it for later use. If you order takeout food, someone will deliver it on real dishes with silverware chopsticks, not in Styrofoam with wooden chopsticks. When you're done eating, place the dishes outside your door and they'll mysteriously disappear by morning. Try the barbecue chicken, but don't be surprised if you discover the chicken's neck and claws are in the box too! Borrow movies from a nearby video rental store. You'll find ten of these stores in a two-mile radius. Take too much time returning the movies and the owners will send their kids to retrieve them. Late fees are considered in poor taste. When you buy cigarettes and beer at one of the many local convenience marts, don't feel chagrined if the person taking your money is a kid in middle school. If you work in Korea, expect to get paid in cash, usually in 10,000 Korean won increments (roughly $10.00 bills). As a courtesy and for your protection, the bank tellers will put your stack of green in a brown paper bag.

Picking Wings Off Butterflies

Apparently, the bag fools would-be robbers, because I never got mugged each month I walked out of the bank clutching a stack of paper bills sealed within their paper safe.

My high school students attended the private school where I taught Monday through Friday from six to eleven in the evenings. At the private institutions students learn advanced geometry, physics, and languages such as Chinese and English. If a family can afford to send only one child to these institutions, it will be the eldest son. If the family can send only one child to the university, it will be the eldest son. To the eldest son falls the responsibility of taking care of his parents when they are too old to take care of themselves. This system must work, because I never saw a nursing home during my stay or a homeless person out on the streets.

The following is a list of general tips for foreigners visiting Korea:

Men don't belong in the kitchen, but some women of the younger generation like it when men volunteer for kitchen duty. Stop talking when the food arrives. Koreans eat fast and usually in silence. Unlike in Western culture, be prepared to sit around talking after dinner for sometimes hours on end. Kimchi is good with every meal and, I believe, more physically addicting than nicotine. I still eat the stinky, spicy cabbage on a regular basis. I've been known to eat it for breakfast. I have a jar in the fridge now. Seriously.

If you're the elder in a group of people at a restaurant, expect to pay for the meal, unless you're a foreign teacher, in which case insist on paying from time to time.

Get used to being stared at, because when strolling city streets, you'll feel like a bright foreign object bobbing about in a sea of black-haired locals.

Learn some of the language, but learn it well. Hangul is a language in which the endings of some words and sentences change when spoken within certain age groups. Using elementary endings when speaking to one's elders is not only disrespectful, but people will think you're babbling like a baby.

Koreans—like many Asians—cherish a concept of personal space that differs from those accepted in Western cultures. For example, while waiting in line at any local bank, in any average American town, one might leave a good six feet between himself and the person at the counter ahead of him. Asians might comfortably cut this space by five feet. I once had a person literally breathing down my neck while paying my electric bill—and we were the only two people standing in line!

Koreans—like Americans and people of virtually every other culture on earth—believe their ways are superior. Expect to be reminded of this fact from time to time.

When you walk through a shopping district one week, expect many of the storefronts to change the following week. Koreans can throw up a new restaurant, a teahouse, a flower shop, or an entire apartment complex seemingly overnight.

The landscaping crew that takes care of the grounds at your apartment may consist of men and women in their sixties and seventies who have yet to be introduced to power equipment.

While driving, watch out for grandmas on mopeds and old men sweeping city streets with huge straw brooms.

Korea is a fascinating place to live and visit. It's a modern country where scenes reminiscent of its ancient history have a way of flashing before your eyes on a daily basis. As much as I regretted leaving Asia, it was time to get back to the life I really wanted.

Upon my return, I discovered that David and Dana had mutated into typical unruly siblings during my absence.

Picking Wings Off Butterflies

They had become mortal enemies, in fact. David terrorized Dana every waking moment he had the chance. Dana even called 911 on him one day. Boys are already prone to antagonizing their little sisters, but David's impulsiveness made him all the more diabolical. His primary goal was to piss her off until she chased him around the house, and then he'd quickly retreat behind closed doors. Frustrated beyond reason, Dana began grabbing the iron poker from the fireplace and, in desperation, tried to tear the doors down to get at him. Nearly every door in the house had been destroyed from their rampages.

I sat them on the couch upon my return and remember thinking that what they really needed was a swift lesson in forgiveness and not punishment. They had been terrors to each other and to their mother. I don't know how Gena managed to work and take care of them during my absence. And after all, doors are just hollow slabs of wood and easily replaced. I knew they were expecting a much harsher punishment for all the bad things they'd done, but we had all done regrettable things. So they looked tremendously relieved after our little chat in which I did absolutely nothing and merely said, "We are all going to forget what happened in the past and start all over again."

This was much easier for the kids to accept than it was for Gena and me. To this day, both of us regret the circumstances that drove us apart. But I say this with a smile knowing our separation catapulted our love for each other far beyond where it might have been had we not separated. Living in Korea enriched me significantly as a person. Gena also had a great time in my absence. She met new friends and explored a different side of life without me looking over her shoulder. On the other hand, there's a popular saying that goes, "We don't know what we've got until it's gone." This saying proved itself true in our situation, because we both came to the realization of how tragic our lives would have been had we not reunited as a family.

Gena and I are a statistical anomaly. The probability that couples who get divorced will be successfully remarried to each other again is slim. Many couples try, but few succeed. Gena and I remarried at our home on May 15, 1999, amid close friends and family. Even my father and mother thought the event too important to pass up. Having divorced when I was nine, they had not set foot in the same state at the same time for decades. We had the ceremony out on the front porch facing the setting sun. Dana was the bridesmaid, and David was the best man. We had the reception on the back deck lit in part by the sunset and the candles floating in our swimming pool. Although we had plenty of parking on the grass surrounding our home, it was the rainy season, and we didn't want our guests to get stuck in the mud. So we hired a limo and driver for the night to shuttle our guests to and from their cars in nearby Pflugerville, Texas. As it turned out, the weather was perfect, and Dana and her friends enjoyed the limo the most by convincing the driver to run them all around town.

Our love might make many couples green with envy, but we earned this love through our commitment to each other's happiness when we could have easily given up. Perhaps more significant, our love grew under the duress brought about by the unique challenges of raising our son. Difficult times and circumstances will erode any relationship. Yet those same circumstances can forge relationships that will never be destroyed no matter how grueling the conditions. This is the depth of love that Gena and I now enjoy: a love that still grows stronger each day.

We have also accomplished much more together during

Picking Wings Off Butterflies

our remarriage than during our previous marriage to each other. After remarrying, we took a huge financial gamble and started a hospice company in Austin. Later we expanded with another branch in La Grange. Gena and I worked side by side during this venture, dividing up responsibilities as they presented themselves. We operated the hospice for three years, and with the help of a wonderful team of individuals we expanded to become one of the largest hospices in Austin. Eventually, we sold them to a nationally known hospice company. I've had many people tell me that they could never work with their spouse, much less spend twenty-four hours a day with them!

CHAPTER 14

LOWERING EXPECTATIONS

*G*ena and I cherished the hope that David would fully recover before he turned eighteen. The German doctors in Frankfurt initially gave him a 30 percent chance of survival and a 100 percent chance of permanent brain damage. These were bad odds. That we were too optimistic is certain, but he had rebounded so quickly after the accident! By the time David entered his teens and high school years, only then did we begin to seriously contemplate having to lower our expectations concerning his recovery.

Still I refused to lose heart. In fact, I was being just as hard on David as ever by still encouraging him to act like other boys his age. I told him often, "I believe in you, David. Even though you think I'm being hard on you and that I don't accept you, I do. The thing is, I believe in you too much to allow even you to accept your shortcomings. See yourself through my eyes."

Picking Wings Off Butterflies

My inability to accept David's handicaps is an unresolved paradox. On the one hand, it was necessary for me to turn a blind eye to his genuine handicaps and to believe that he could "will" himself to get better. But on the other hand, my insistence that he can get better despite his handicaps probably makes him feel as if he will never measure up to my expectations. He likely interprets my frustration incorrectly and will never fully understand how much I love him.

This, in fact, is my greatest difficulty: accepting David for who he is, right now, in all his broken glory.

For many of us, much of our dissatisfaction with life is caused by our inability to become what we aspire to be. We see our future and the perfection of our capabilities. We place cutout pictures of ourselves in the life collage of our choosing. But most of us will fail in reaching our imagined potentialities, having been snared in the net of mediocrity. How is it with a broken mind? Within the intricate web of the psyche, where do aspiration, motivation, fortitude, and optimism dwell? Did these abilities once reside in the dark globules illuminated by the X-rays of David's scull? Have these powers been rendered useless? Or are these abilities lurking somewhere in his brain, still capable of being ignited by our hopes as his parents?

Throughout the years David was in school he visited and lived in several inpatient and outpatient facilities. I recall no less than six facilities, one of which was halfway across the country. You can't just look up one of these places in the yellow pages and drop your troubled teen at the door. Most people don't even know these kinds of places are around, because the facilities often look like country clubs. Patients are usually referred to these facilities and can wait months or years to get in. As you'd expect, they're pricey, but there's often financial aid for those who need it.

In caring for David, we considered these treatment facilities as a last resort. We preferred David to be with us and have as normal a life as possible. When we did escort David through the doors of these facilities, we did so to preserve our own sanity, and because David was going through difficult-enough times to require twenty-four-hour monitoring. It wasn't like David had been acting up for several days and we got fed up with him. David's rough patches spanned months. We did everything humanly possible for him during these periods and for as long as possible before acknowledging that he needed specialized care. Only then, after everything we tried had failed, did we pack his bags.

Between the times David resided at treatment facilities, there were visits to dozens of counselors who helped David work through many of his issues. There were also many trips to psychiatrists, primarily to obtain prescriptions and monitor his medications. Through the years of endless psychiatric visits, I'm certain Gena and I earned the equivalent of a master's degree in psychology. Together, we have learned every trick in the book, tried all the latest treatments, and became familiar with every drug and strategy to help our son. When picking new counselors and psychiatrists, we asked ourselves two fundamental questions: What does this professional know that we don't already know? What will this professional try that we haven't already tried?

As a strange side effect of going to these facilities and visiting professionals, David learned ingenious ways of acting mentally disturbed. To this day, he's still learning these tactics. David has also been known to develop psychological problems simply by learning such problems exist. This is downright disconcerting, and an ongoing occurrence, which makes it difficult to distinguish David's real problems from his imaginary ones.

One day, David pranced out of a session into the waiting area filled with people and asked me if I'd heard the ruckus he made in the counselor's office.

"Nope. Sorry. What happened?"

"I went crazy in there. I started screaming, and they had to come and hold me down."

"You were perfectly fine when you went in. Why'd you go crazy?"

"Because I thought the cops were coming to get me."

David does have a lot on his plate these days, what with being arrested and the fact that police officers petrify him. The counselor he's seeing is a nice young man who's genuinely helping David work through his problems. He's as green as a leprechaun, though, and too inexperienced to know the difference between David's real issues and the ones he fakes to get attention. David had never gone berserk in any facility before. Somehow he got the idea in his head that if he acted crazy, then he would not be sent to jail. While going berserk was a new behavior for David this time, it showed how David's problems have multiplied through years of continued exposure to—ironically—the places, professionals, and treatment plans best equipped to solve his problems.

Not everyone who has a brain injury is interested in mimicking symptoms of real illnesses to sabotage his own personal growth. David just happens to enjoy doing it, and he's gotten pretty good at it. My opinion is that David is extremely intelligent in the fine art of manipulation. He knows how to push buttons to get people to believe he's incapable of doing something he's actually quite capable of doing himself. I realize this isn't a positive thing to say about my son, but it's true. He knows he has this skill. His family knows he has this skill. What he's yet to figure out is that he's not fooling anyone.

I mention this because it has a direct bearing on my expectations for David. He's capable of doing a lot with his life, but he's yet to harness the motivation. He'd prefer that people do things for him. Just about anyone will help someone who can't help himself. Some will help when they recognize that the person asking for help is at least trying to help himself. But most of us don't have the patience to help those whom we know are manipulating us. This is called enabling. The challenge with David is knowing when to push him when he's being lazy and when to help him when he honestly can't help himself due to his handicaps.

To illustrate, David's newest favorite expression is "It didn't occur to me." It's almost equivalent to a politician saying, "I don't recall." This expression is symptomatic of my challenge in knowing what David can and cannot do. There are a lot of things that just don't occur to David, because frankly, there are a lot of things in his brain that are *not occurring*. One of three phenomena seems to be happening within his mind: First, he lacks certain mental abilities, because the parts of his brain that make these abilities work no longer function. In other words, when he says something didn't occur to him, it's possible the thought never crossed his mind. Second, even when it does occur to him to do something, it's quite possible he's lost the ability either physically or emotionally to carry out the task altogether. Third—and this provides insight into his motivation and core personality—it's possible that his brain is functioning optimally regarding the carrying out of most skills, but it just doesn't occur to him to complete a task because he has

Picking Wings Off Butterflies

no desire to, because he simply doesn't think the task is interesting or important.

"David, do you know why there are times when I can be angry with you all through the day?" I asked him a few weeks ago.

"No."

"It's because I have to keep telling you things over and over."

"Really?" he asked, looking guilty.

"I went to use the restroom, and when I lifted the lid, it was drenched with your piss."

"I wiped it off!" he argued.

David's not that steady on his toes, and nine times out of ten, he will urinate on the toilet lid. Kids will do this, and uncaring adults still do. He's been drenching the seat since the accident, and now that he's living with me, I prefer he learn the skill of urinating through the opening of the toilet. After years and years of hassling him, I've never been able to train him to lift the lid, but he has learned to wipe off the top of the seat.

"David, what do you think is easier? Reaching down and lifting the lid before you pee, or spending five minutes after you pee cleaning up your mess?"

"It's easier to wipe the lid off," he told me. He will argue against the obvious, because he doesn't like to admit when he's wrong.

In deciding how best to counsel David, however, I have to consider what might be going on in his mind. Perhaps the thought actually doesn't occur in his brain that pissing all over the toilet is rude. Maybe the thought occurs to him, but he's not able to carry out the function of either getting his aim right or lifting the lid. But it could just be that he has lower standards and doesn't care about pissing all over the toilet in the first place. As usual, I err on the side of believing David is fully capable of completing this task, as well as many other simple routines. He simply chooses not to. Which tells me he's capable of doing a lot of things.

Here are a few more examples. David sucked his thumb into his high school years. Gena and I are familiar with every conceivable, foolproof, anti–thumb sucking technique ever invented. About the only thing we didn't try was coating his thumbs with habanero pepper extract. Don't let anyone tell you otherwise, nothing works to stop thumb sucking. Like the common cold, what works best is time. Just wait until it occurs to the child to stop, which in David's case took much longer than most. Speaking as a father, I can assure you that watching my ninth-grade son suck his thumb was quite distressing.

Even into his early twenties, David would wipe his hands on his shirt regardless of what was on them. Who needs napkins at mealtimes when you're wearing a nice shirt? He'd also use his shirt collar to wipe his nose and face. Let's just say this made it virtually impossible for me to give the lad a warm hug. When your kid is a toddler and covered in body fluids, your arms can reach around the mess. What's more, you're bigger. After you give him a hug, you can pick him up by the belt and toss him in the bathtub. But when your child weighs as much as you do, and he's just as filthy as a toddler, then he's not so cute and cuddly. And David likes to hug. To this day, he's insecure and clingy.

During the on and off times that David has lived with us, I often have to get on my hands and knees with a rag and wipe coffee spills off the floor. David drinks coffee from morning until night. One standing rule I have for him that he observes (but only when I'm around) is that he can drink coffee only in the kitchen and dining room. These rooms are tiled. I enforce this rule, because every time David makes a cup of coffee, he fills it to the brim and spills drops of coffee wherever he walks. After a decade, I've given up telling him to leave space between the coffee and the top of the cup. It's far less stressful for me if I keep my mouth shut and hand-mop the kitchen floor after him.

After we moved to Alaska, Dana, David, and I were driving down the road in my truck one day. I don't recall what the conversation was about, but it must have been about cleanliness.

David said, "I haven't washed my face since I was eight years old."

I glanced at him sitting in the passenger seat and paraphrased the unbelievable comment. "You haven't washed your face in almost fifteen years?"

"Yeah."

"Why, David?" Dana asked.

"I heard soap was bad for your face. So I don't use it on my face anymore."

"But you do use it on the rest of your body—right?" I asked.

"Yeah," he replied with uncertainty.

"I don't understand. How do you keep your face clean?" I asked. I'd never seen a pimple on his face—ever.

"Well, when I wash my hair, the shampoo rinses my face."

At that moment, I thought the kid just came up with a new anti-pimple remedy that could make us all filthy (pun intended) rich.

David urinates frequently as though it were a perpetual emergency. Three to four times an hour is common and sometimes every ten minutes. Right before we leave on any trip, he'll go to the bathroom two or three times in a five-minute span. His goal is to get it all out, because if the trip lasts more than fifteen minutes, he'll be in a lot of pain, and so will we when we have to deal with his frantic cries of "pull over!" Any trip can turn into a nightmare, and most do.

David had the opportunity to correct this problem, but true to form, he made the problem worse. A physician finally diagnosed David with diabetes insipidus. It's a disease accentuated by his head injury. It's not serious, but it has at least one annoying symptom: frequent urination. We didn't know David had this form of diabetes. What we knew was that David had a urination problem, caused solely by his accident, but we couldn't convince any doctor that there was a connection between the two in order for him to be treated. That was until the appointment with a more knowledgeable physician. She recommended David use a medicated nasal inhaler, and he was ordered to drink less fluids. Now all David had to do was use the inhaler once before bedtime and cut down a little on his fluid intake. Presto! A medical mystery that has plagued him and his family for eighteen years solved. What did David do? The opposite. He tripled his fluid intake, and it didn't "occur" to him to use the medicated inhaler.

David's never been a big fan of taking his medications on a regular basis anyway. I understand this to be common among individuals who are mentally disabled. We can yell at him and counsel him about how much happier we would all be if he just took his meds. To be entirely candid, getting David to take his meds is a battle I disengaged from a long time ago. In fact, I don't fight with David anymore about anything to convince him what's in his best interest. He no longer listens to me. I wait for that miraculous moment when it will occur to David to start taking care of himself.

Picking Wings Off Butterflies

Okay, now to be entirely forthright. Gena, Dana, and I have always been there for David. We will always be there, standing in his corner, rooting for him. And we must always be there for David, because nobody else will be.

On the last day of 2006, our family went to a New Year's Eve party. I found Gena after dinner talking with a woman whose young teenage son was giving her a lot of grief. I always listen intently when parents talk about their relationships with their children. Her son was about twelve years of age. She said that he didn't listen to her anymore, that he just wanted to play video games, and that he was refusing to do his homework and chores. She was adamant; if her child did not straighten up pronto, she would kick him out of the house before he hit puberty.

Most parents can relate to her frustration. Parents can handle only so much parent-child conflict before they need a time-out away from their own kids. I'm wondering when Gena and I lost our sanity. This is certainly nothing to gloat over, and I don't want to appear insensitive, but we've been through things with David that would have given many a parent a nervous breakdown. It's not an option for us to kick David out of the house. It's not an option for us to abandon him even though he turned eighteen more than seven years ago. It will never be an option for us to *not* take care of him in some way. When David was born, we didn't expect to be caring for him well into *his* sixties. But I can now visualize myself wiping his coffee stains off my kitchen floor and cleaning up after him after he uses my bathroom well into *my* eighties!

Does David aspire to be a certain kind of man? Does he have the tenacity to see his dreams fulfilled? Were these desires damaged in the accident? If damaged, to what degree? These are the questions I constantly wrestle with in my daily assessment of what David can and cannot do. The only reasonable conclusion I can draw is that David is fully functioning in many ways, but he's not functioning with a purpose that will bring him a better quality of life.

Are my expectations of David unfounded? In other words, do I expect David to have the same attitude toward life that I have? Do the expectations of fathers for their sons—and conversely, the expectations of sons toward their fathers—ever meet? Of course not. There's a generation gap, a personality gap, an intelligence or experience gap, and a million other gaps in which we all have to admit that our children might never measure up to our expectations. Nor should they.

I don't know what kind of man David would have become had he not been injured. Most fathers have this luxury, because they can control the factors that contribute to what their sons will become. They can teach and lead, encourage certain hobbies and interests, even help choose or pay for educational pursuits. I certainly tried to shape David's future, but my goals proved futile. As I've explained, I never know how much I can expect from David. Ultimately, I can't crawl inside his head and see what's broken inside his mind. If I could, I might discover there are certain dynamics of his brain that don't function at the level that would allow David to accomplish what he wants to accomplish. On the other hand, all of the components in his brain that are required to make him successful might be working with the exception of say, motivation. But is a lack of motivation really a character flaw? For that matter, if a person chooses not to follow society's guidelines on how to be successful, is this a character defect?

My take on this is that, as parents, we expect too much from our children, especially if we've accomplished a lot in our own lives. I suspect this holds true for parents all over the world in every known culture. It's possible, even if David had not had his accident, that he would have led an average existence anyway. He might have been the kind of person who doesn't care whether his clothes and apartment are ever clean. He might have always despised getting a formal education. He might have never cared about working his way up a company ladder. Maybe he would have been the artistic type, a person driven by his passions or idealism, rather than by financial success. Who knows? My point is, how much should I care about what *I* want David to be as opposed to what *he* wants to be?

A partial answer: Deep down, I had certain expectations when I raised David. Why? Because this is what's expected of parents. And children who are raised by moms and dads who care enough to help guide in their future often turn out to be much like their parents. My expectations of what David could do simply parallel the expectations I placed on myself. But I also have an ulterior motive. I need David to become capable of financially supporting himself so I don't have to foot the bill for the rest of his life.

What I am learning, both dutifully and refreshingly, is to lower the bar and expect less from David. This is not because he doesn't measure up to my expectations, but because my expectations of what it means to have a successful and meaningful life must fall more in line with reality. For we are all different and, in certain respects, broken. Some of us are broken at birth, some by accident, and many are wounded on the battleground of life. We are all successful to varying degrees, because no matter where we begin or what happens to us in life, we all have to overcome obstacles to become the kind of person we want to become.

CHAPTER 15

SURVIVING ADOLESCENCE

My friend Martin. This person was the best friend I ever had. He probably was the only person who accepted me for what I was. We were different. He was, in a nice way of saying, a prep, or geeky. I was a person who was into things he would never have involved himself with, and I was somewhat respected for it at that time. This is the reason why whenever I saw that Martin was being picked on I stood up for him and told the person who was bothering him to back off, and they would listen.

Martin was a smart person, but was unable to get his point across to people when he was fed up with all that was being said or done to him. He'd yell at people, but nobody listened. I didn't like that. I know how it feels to be picked on, and so I would stick up for him. Me and Martin had ideas to do something that would be a career for us, and we would talk about it a lot. Unfortunately, his life was taken from him in a car accident his junior summer vacation. But if it had not been taken, we would have done things with our ideas.

You can't beat time. We all have a deadline. Nineteen years was all he got, and I'll never forget him. He was the one person I've known that did not change his appearance or his lifestyle to some passing trend and that's something to respect. I could not go that far. By then I was much obsessed with being respected by mischievous people to care about changing.

When we told David the news that his best friend Martin had died, we could see a gloomy feeling of emptiness take over his countenance. It was the first time I realized that David genuinely cared for somebody else. Up until then, David had always been absorbed in his obsessive pursuit of self-gratification. He picked friends for what they could do for him, not the other way around. This is what kids do—and what some adults still do—until they discover that true friendship requires taking an interest in learning about the lives of those whom they wish to befriend. Through the death of his friend, David showed me he could think of other people's needs more than his own. He wondered about the physical pain Martin might have gone through in the accident, and he also thought about what Martin's parents might have been feeling after the death of their son. This was true empathy.

David and Martin had big ideas for their future. They were working on a Transformers-type cartoon, with plans to spin off their ideas into action figures of their own design. It's wonderful how children have the ability to create their own worlds and imaginary successes. As we get older and lose our sense of wonder we begin to make up excuses as to why our plans won't work in the real world. Martin's death killed the plans David set for himself. He's made other plans since then, such as becoming an artist or a musician, but I haven't seen David exhibit the enthusiasm needed to carry out those plans like he had before his friend died.

Throughout David's years in school, he experienced the benefits, as well as the disadvantages, of utilizing the special education system. Our experience was that special education really equated to receiving a great education in elementary and middle school. During those years, David learned targeted academics in smaller classroom settings in which the teacher-to-student ratio usually numbered one to ten. His teachers were also specially trained and extraordinarily patient in motivating and encouraging students with a wide variety of special considerations. David also rode special education buses with drivers and assistant drivers who were all trained to meet the needs of children with specific handicaps.

These exceptions and special considerations began to taper off in high school, but this was probably for the better. During his high school years, David was integrated into regular classes attended by otherwise normal children, and when his academics didn't meet the bar, he needed to attend special education classes for certain subjects. When it came to mathematics, for example, David wasn't attending regular algebra or calculus classes; he was attending the most basic of math courses, which were often attended by students with learning disabilities. Yet, in the case of social studies and history, David joined regular classroom settings. David was also provided with tutors, and helpers who would walk him from class to class. He also received certain breaks and accommodations, such as being given more time to finish homework and exams.

For half of his senior year, David was required to attend a generic classroom environment where teachers babysat students with disciplinary problems. Since David was already highly susceptible to mimicking inappropriate behavior, this was the worst classroom environment for him. Suddenly David's homework turned from legitimately challenging assignments to juvenile math and English worksheets, much of which resembled academics he had breezed through back in the fourth grade. I'm not sure whether David was giving up on himself or whether the school system was giving up on David. Perhaps it was a little bit of both. Academically, David had begun following the path of least resistance. To his own detriment, he had hooked up with other kids who were not known for exhibiting exemplary behavior. If I put myself in the shoes of the school officials, I really couldn't blame them for isolating the kids who did not want to learn from those who did. Either way, we were frustrated when it appeared that the school system seemed to be merely pushing David through to graduation.

When we saw the quality of David's education slipping, we fought even harder for his rights as a student with special needs. With help from school administrators, we got David enrolled in a work-study program. This meant David would attend school in the mornings, which allowed him to complete his diploma, and he would go to work in the afternoons, which provided him with employment, as well as the opportunity to develop socialization skills. After David's morning classes, a school bus would take him to an electronics manufacturing plant about twenty miles from home. Heavily supervised, David worked the next four hours doing odd jobs such as moving supplies and boxes, taking out the trash, and assembly-line work. He even got cash to put in his chain wallet. The downside of the whole deal was that Gena or I had to pick David up at the plant every night of the workweek. This took about an hour and a half out of our evenings, driving through some of the worst traffic in Austin. But David absolutely flourished with this arrangement. The semester he was in the program has been the most productive year of his life thus far. His self-esteem shot through the roof.

When David succeeded in this program, I knew he had a future. He was literally working a twelve-hour day by juggling the demands of school and work. He got up at seven every morning, Monday through Friday, and we didn't get home until seven at night. It's difficult for most adults to stay focused and work this hard. For David, this was a major achievement. You see, ever since his accident, we had been wondering how well he was going to navigate high school. We could now visualize that he was not only going to graduate, but upon graduation, he was also going to have the ability to take on full-time employment. Just maybe he could even pull off going to college and make a real future for himself!

Boy, were we wrong.

When I got into high school I wanted to be accepted as a cool kid, so I evolved from someone who was scared to be left out to someone who was welcomed with open arms. I wore baggy clothes with wallet chains. I wore earrings in both ears. I swore all the time. I started using drugs. I became dependent on cigarettes. I stayed out late, skipped school, was sent to the office all the time, and I was terrible at home because of my wanting to be accepted.

I agree. *You were a little hellion, David.*

But I must digress and consider my own high school years...

In Tucson, Arizona, I attended an experimental high

Picking Wings Off Butterflies

school called Project MORE. The time period was the seventies. Perhaps you can imagine how laid back this school must have been. At Project MORE, I called my teachers by their first names, like Bill, my science teacher, and Liz, my social studies teacher. Few of my classes had real chairs, so students usually sat in beanbag chairs or on the carpet. Few rooms even had doors, and I recall entering at least one room by parting a curtain of beaded, psychedelic streamers. Not only could I bring cigarettes to school, but I also could leave my pack out in the open, like in my shirt pocket or sitting next to me on my worktable while attending classes—that is, when I did attend. There were no bells to signal when it was time to go to class. The school was housed in a 1950s two-story office building near downtown and was sandwiched between a street and railroad tracks. I recall a skinny hallway on both floors that ran the entire length of the building and parted the building in half with rooms lined up on both sides. I often skateboarded from one end of the hallway to the other. I didn't wear baggy clothes, but what I usually wore were cutoff jean shorts and a T-shirt. My attire was nowhere near as weird as one tribe of kids at school who sported medieval outfits complete with chain-mesh shirts and purple velvet capes. I also carried a tattered, home-sewn denim bag over my shoulder. My friends and I often ditched classes to go skate, and before leaving school, I'd buy a box lunch and extra oranges. My lunch, my smokes, a bit of illegal contraband, and any other crap I might have been carrying had to go somewhere, and the hippie purse worked great. I often wore a pair of custom-made Kaibab Indian moccasins that came up to my knees.

When I reflect on the similarities of when David and I went through high school—even though a generation separated us—I sense we shared a lot of the same characteristics. We desperately wanted to be unique—if not eccentric—as we both aspired to be accepted by who we thought were the cool kids. So we adapted our attire and mannerisms to differentiate us from the kids we thought belonged to the average Joes. I suppose this was because we wanted to distinguish ourselves as originals. We both wore strange clothes suitable for the time. I carried a hippie purse and wore Indian moccasins. David sported a wallet attached with a thirty-pound dog chain that pulled his pants down to his knees. We swore all the time. We drank a little. We became addicted to cigarettes. We were nonconformists. We didn't like the rigidity of the school environment, skipped school, and did pretty much the opposite of what everyone thought we should be doing.

Like father like son, I guess, but with a few notable exceptions...

I was not into piercing my body in every conceivable location. Girls wore earrings when I went to high school, not guys. David started piercing many parts of his anatomy such as his eyebrows and tongue. Why anyone wants a barbell bouncing between their teeth and slurring their speech is beyond me. I thought David was "going mental," when, in fact, he was quite normal for his time. He'd say I was old-fashioned, and he'd be right. Still, there were times he looked like a gothic crypt keeper. We'd have knock-down, drag-out verbal fights because of his appearance and the way he carried himself. Frankly, Gena and I were embarrassed to go out in public with him.

Today's younger generation still insists on wearing baggy pants and chains. Why wear pants that mop up the mud as they drag across the ground? Why walk with your legs spread apart looking as though you are constipated? I have to laugh when I see petty thieves caught by the cops on

Picking Wings Off Butterflies

television because their britches are falling down and they couldn't run away! And using industrial-sized dog chains to hold wallets in place, which are likely just filled with cigarette money or a wishful condom, seems overkill anyway. Peer pressure is powerful. Kids from every generation will go to a lot of trouble to fit in with their classmates. And twenty years maturer, most of us will look back with horror at the way we looked and acted in our teens.

I smoked marijuana at times, and unlike certain political candidates, I inhaled. I tried a few other drugs, but never understood what the hoopla was all about. I hated drinking ever since the first time I got drunk after drinking a pint of Jim Beam in the eighth grade. I felt like dying and was lucky I didn't get alcohol poisoning. Eventually, I quit smoking pot when I was eighteen and started skating professionally in California on the vertical roller skating circuit. I didn't want to take a serious fall while skating, and I was starting to prefer being free of strange intoxicants influencing my thoughts. From what I know, David experimented with different drugs than the ones I did, because the drugs floating around his school were not concocted in the seventies. But I probably wouldn't have taken today's modern drugs anyway—too risky. In the world we live in, even trick-or-treaters at Halloween run the risk of some insane person messing with their candy. You think I'm going to trust a drug dealer to care about quality control and what goes into my body? Hell no!

David took a few guilty strolls to the principal's office, and I attended many parent-teacher conferences due to his behavior. I was not a model student, but my delinquent behavior must have slipped under the radar, because I never got in trouble at school. David graduated from high school. I didn't. I dropped out in my senior year. I was living with my mother and sister at the time in a neighborhood where Joe Dirt might have lived. I got tired of watching my mom drag herself home at night working for minimum wage. Within a week of dropping out, I had a full-time job cooking at a nearby restaurant buffet to help support our family. I've been working ever since. Only later did I wise up, get my GED, and go on to earn a bachelor's degree. Last time I counted, I've had roughly thirty jobs, including more than a handful of businesses. Not wanting to ever be that poor again, I expect to always be motivated by poverty-paranoia and have two or three sources of income cooking away on the back burners.

So, when I swap high school stories with David, I'm not sure who shakes out to be the biggest winner—or loser. We both screwed up, both missed opportunities, both gained experiences that we don't regret. Still, I'm certain David gave Gena and me far more grief than I ever gave my parents.

One evening, we sent David down to the supermarket to get a half-gallon carton of ice cream. I let him drive my own truck, a green Dodge Dakota that Gena bought me for Christmas while we were living in San Antonio. She surprised me at my work by pulling up in the beauty punctuated with a huge red bow attached to the antenna! Anyway, David was running pretty late when there was a knock on the door. He had wrecked the truck a mile down the road. The person at the door had given him a ride home after pulling him out of the driver's-side window.

"Surely it can't be that bad?" I asked David.

After all, he was standing right in front of me without a scratch on him. David just kind of stood there . . . shaking. We drove down the street to a point where the road swung around a gentle curve, and we saw the tail end of the truck pinned in a row of trees.

Picking Wings Off Butterflies

David said, "I looked down, looked up, panicked, hit the accelerator instead of the brakes, spun off the road to the left, cleared the ditch, did a full three-sixty, and plowed into those trees."

Gena and I didn't learn our lesson that David should not be driving. We bought him a used Saturn a year after he totaled the truck. Months passed with no calamities, until there came another knock on the door. The officer informed us that someone had written down David's license plate number after he bumped into another car in a grocery store parking lot. We pressed David about other possible driving infractions and learned more than we wanted. This was not the first time he'd been involved in a little fender bender and skedaddled like nothing happened, and there were also other instances when he played chicken with shopping carts and used the Saturn to go four-wheeling through the Texas countryside.

One fine day, David even drove into the supporting column of our two-car garage and nearly collapsed the roof. Repairs ran a thousand bucks. After the incident, I checked out the inside of his car and saw that he'd shredded the foam on the ceiling panel. I guess he thought he was Michelangelo at the Sistine Chapel, but the figures David carved out with a razor blade were not angelic. The etchings portrayed skulls, crossbones, snakes, and the names of popular metal bands. Gena and I finally faced the inevitable truth: it was not safe for David to drive a car.

Despite all that happened to David in high school, he would survive adolescence and, more importantly, graduate from high school. Through the years, I'd grown weary of pestering his teachers and school administrators to make sure he got the best education possible. Upon his graduation, I was just grateful he'd managed to get his diploma, which is more than I can say I accomplished myself. My GED was good enough to get me into college. David was not bound for college (as far as we knew), but I also figured that his poor grades would not prevent him from getting a basic job anyway. What mattered was that David had in his fist the one piece of paper that was proof to the world that he was capable of reaching higher goals.

CHAPTER 16

"NORTH TO THE FUTURE!"

When we moved to the sleepy town of Pflugerville in 1997, it was the best kept secret in Texas. After exiting I-35, I could coast through town and be at our home in the country in less than fifteen minutes. As a suburb north of Austin, Pflugerville grew exponentially after we discovered its charm. I didn't tell a soul, but I swear half of Austin followed us there.

We were now anxious to experience entirely new adventures. With the kids out of high school, it seemed the best time to move and throw on a different coat. In actuality, we had never made the decision to officially live in Texas. We were "ordered" to San Antonio by the army after David's accident. We stayed in Texas because there was work. Only later did we wonder if we'd gotten stuck there, and when you feel stuck, you have to move to get your circulation going. Selling the two hospice businesses we'd built put a little money in our pocket, at least enough to start a new life somewhere else. One thing led to another until one day we were driving through southwest Utah. We liked the beauty of the area, went on a whirlwind house-hunting safari for four days, and bought a house in a place called Ivins located just northwest of St. George.

A few months later, the movers packed our stuff in Texas and away we went. I pulled our travel trailer with my pickup. Our pet parakeet rode in the trailer in a cage, and our young German shepherd, Fritz, rode in his kennel in the bed of my truck. (Regrettably, Sheeba had passed away, and we buried her on the hill in our backyard overlooking the stream.) Gena drove her Toyota. We packed Dana's things in her own truck and strapped her dog, Cassie, in the front seat. Whenever Dana passed me on the highway, I saw Cassie sitting up with her tongue out of her mouth and head bobbing about, gazing toward a world of wonder she'd never seen before. My mother took turns giving Gena and Dana a break from driving, and David bounced around between all three vehicles, keeping us all company. Walkie-talkies kept the boredom down, especially through the isolated desert stretches of West Texas and New Mexico.

The beauty of the desert ignites the soul. I first experienced the Southwest after moving to Tucson, Arizona, from Hawaii. In high school at the time, I often awakened early in the morning while the sky was still pitch black. I'd scale the side fence attached to the garage of the humble home my mom had purchased; sit on the cold, gritty crest of the roof; and wait for the sunrise to pop over the Rincon Mountains to the east. I was never disappointed by the show. It would begin with the slightest hint of blue on the horizon, peak with successive waves of fiery red clouds rippling across the sky, and culminate with fainting yellowish clouds

Picking Wings Off Butterflies

blossoming like puffs of smoke within a maya-blue sky. It was a sight to behold.

To me, Utah is by far the prettiest state for those who love the mystique of the West. The home we picked out in Ivins was right smack in the midst of the best of any desert environment. From our front door we could be in Zion National Park in less than an hour, the north rim of the Grand Canyon in two and a half hours, and Bryce Canyon in three. We were a fifteen-minute walk from Snow Canyon State Park, which is a gorgeous, sandstone-terraced canyon pixilated in reds rivaling Sedona, Arizona. When we drove north out of Snow Canyon, we could be in cool mountain pines in less than twenty minutes after passing a number of cinder-crusted volcanic cones. Las Vegas was a short hour and a half drive doing seventy-five.

Once we settled into the area, Gena took a job working as the general manager of a hospice in St. George, and I worked on the house. The home we purchased didn't have landscaping in the backyard, and the basement was unfinished. I had a pool put in, and it took me about six months to complete the landscaping around the pool. After finishing the backyard, I set out to remodel our basement, which was a full 1,800 square feet. When I began in the basement, there was nothing but an outer concrete wall and a few supporting walls. When I finished, we had two homes in one. I put in two bedrooms, a library, a living room, a full bath, and a studio-style kitchen. This took me about a year, doing most of the work on my own and contracting out what was beyond my skills. I finished just in time for Dana and Stix to move in.

Dana met Stix while attending a massage school in St. George. The two of them later earned their national certification in massage therapy. I first met Stix when he knocked on my door holding a cardboard box filled with exotic cacti. He'd taken cuttings from cacti growing in his friend's front yard, and I transplanted them in my backyard. I thought he was out to impress me. After all, this is what real gentlemen do when they're seeking permission to marry your daughter. Stix went about courtship the old-fashioned way. One afternoon when I was sitting on my back patio, he asked me for Dana's hand in marriage. I consented, of course, and I was excited for Dana, because she'd found someone to share her life with. Had I known what was to transpire next, I might not have been so quick to accept this particular young man. The reason is, after I offered my consent, Stix moved his zoo into my house.

The animals began arriving in pairs, and then in multiples, filling my empty shop room off the garage to capacity. He brought two African tortoises (which spent most of the time burrowing holes in my backyard), two frilled dragons, a sick savannah monitor, a huge albino python affectionately known as Leeloo (named after the female character in the movie *The Fifth Element*), live rabbits awaiting a whack on the head to feed the python, a pair of chameleons, (which, in a short period of time, spawned three litters and approximately eighty other chameleons), and a huge aquarium filled to the brim with fish, frogs, and water turtles. Fortunately, Stix found a home for his alligator a few months earlier. Stix fed most of his critters crickets, half of which escaped the reptilian jaws they were intended to edify and eventually found their way into every square inch of my shop. My master bedroom was next to the shop, and the chirping of the crickets reverberated in my eardrums all night long and made me think I was camped out in a Louisiana swamp.

Dana and Stix married on Maui on May 10, 2005. Gena

Picking Wings Off Butterflies

and I, along with Stix's father and mother, attended their informal ceremony. Dana's not a fan of big crowds. She opted for the Maui wedding as a quiet alternative. The evening was perfect. Normally around sunset the trade winds are whipping through the valley created by the head and shoulder outline of Maui's coastline. But the trade wind god must have been smiling on the young couple that day, because the evening they married he was breathless.

David looks up to Stix like an older brother—literally. Stix towers six foot two, and David tops out at five foot five. My mother was short, and David inherited this genetic predisposition. David's injuries also contributed to him being shorter than he might have been. I suppose I could add a "short people" complex to David's laundry list of ailments. Stix has been great with David, and in a way he has become David's older brother.

If there exists any lingering animosity between David and his sister, it's due to the fact that David gets depressed when he recognizes Dana is surpassing him in life. Not that he's resentful and hurtful, he's just mindful that life is passing him by, and he feels he has so little to show for his own existence.

When we first moved to Ivins, my mother was in her fifth year of battling cancer. She'd moved out of our home and was living in her own apartment nearby (the apartment David drove to on his moped when he was trying to escape the bully), but she still needed a lot of support. We encouraged her to use hospice services, but she was stubborn. She equated getting on hospice to giving up on her will to live. We all helped her as much as we could. I drove her to her chemo and radiation treatments, back and forth to the pharmacy, made grocery runs, and did tons of other stuff. When she was feeling up to it, she'd come over to our house on the weekends. Gena helped monitor her medications, took the time to consult with her physicians about her care, and helped clean her apartment. Dana and Stix visited her as well. David was living at his own apartment nearby, and he'd ride his moped over to her place, and the two of them would sit together to drink coffee, smoke, and watch television. When needed, he'd zip over to the corner store to buy her more cigarettes. When Grandma didn't answer her phone, we all worried, and one of us would drive over to her house to make sure she'd not taken a bad fall or fallen permanently asleep.

Last saw my mom alive when I rolled her in a wheelchair to the security checkpoint at the Las Vegas airport. Gena and I—once again—were sensing the need to make another move. We'd visited Alaska three times the year before and decided that Alaska might offer the slower pace to life that we were looking for. Although my mother had been battling cancer for many years, she still possessed an incredible tenacity to live. She could well have battled cancer another decade. My mother decided that she did not want to make the move northward. The climate was too cold, and no doubt she was weary of our frantic way of life. She had lived with us on and off for seventeen years, and she could not bear to be the weight preventing us from moving on with our lives. So we made arrangements for her to go live with her brother and his wife in Nebraska. When I left her at the security checkpoint, she was on her way to stay with them.

One fear people often express when thinking about losing someone they love is that they will forget; that time will eventually erase the pictures they have snapped in their minds and the memories of the times shared. I still remember my mother's expression when I left her. The memory is as vivid as looking at a crisp, glossy photograph

Picking Wings Off Butterflies

of her today. We both suspected it would be the last time we'd see each other. We circumvented the pain of our last moments together by pretending we were saying good-bye, much like I often said good-bye while dropping her off at the door to her apartment. She smiled as she looked up at me, but her expression was typical of what one would expect from their own mother. She had this look . . . a look that said, "Don't worry about me. It will be all right. Thank you for all that you have done. Perhaps I'll see you again."

I got lost on the way out of the terminal. My escape routes eluded me in the swirl of faceless people and the clanging of slot machines. I forgot which corridor led to the parking garage. I could hardly see through the blur in my eyes. I don't remember the drive home.

A few weeks later, she took a tumble down a flight of stairs. She'd been wandering around my uncle's house in the early morning hours, probably on her way to the kitchen to grab a snack, when she stumbled down the basement staircase. She fractured her leg, and an ambulance took her to the hospital. The trauma pushed her over the edge, and she passed away a few weeks later.

I could not escape the feeling that her death was partly my fault. There were no stairs in her apartment in St. George. If she'd stayed, she would not have fallen down any stairs. Could we have continued to live in Utah, at least long enough until she died of more natural causes? Of course we could have. Then again, we had been taking care of her for almost two decades. If we had not been taking such good care of her, she may have died much sooner. Then again, had she not lived with us for so many years, we all could have grieved less when she died. Conversely, had she not lived with us for so many years, we all would have loved less and been loved less. I recognize this all sounds confusing, but the volley of thoughts, which arises from second-guessing what we did or did not do regarding those whom we have loved and lost, is natural. There's just so much more I wanted to tell her, so much more I wanted to do with her. Could I have been a better son? Maybe. Maybe not. I tell myself it's not good to beat myself up over what I did or did not do on her behalf. As the years pass, so too does the guilt.

With my mother's passing, Gena and I were able to move on with our lives. What we wanted—what we all needed—was to move on. Gena had quit her job as the general manager of the hospice she was working for. Having operated her own hospices, she found it difficult doing the same line of work for another organization, which didn't offer her the freedom to manage in a way that brought her previous success. Upon graduating from massage school, Dana and Stix had made a valiant but unsuccessful effort at finding massage clients in a city already flooded with an overabundance of massage therapists. To succeed, they would have to go elsewhere. I'd recently completed my second book and had finished the home-remodeling projects. The improvements greatly increased the value of our property. The time to sell was ripe. And then there was David.

He was still getting pulled over by the police on a consistent basis. I was still logging the events down and filling in the answers to the five Ws: Who stopped you? What for? When and where did they stop you? And why can't they just pick on someone who doesn't have a brain injury? The process was getting old. One day an officer even saw David standing on the balcony of his second-floor apartment, and the officer took the time to get out of his squad car, ascend a flight of stairs, and ask for identification to see if he was old enough to smoke. For whatever the reasons—none noble or justified—the force was continuing to target my brain-injured son.

Another day, David got hauled into police headquarters for supposedly stealing an item out of a motel room. A witness said that the suspect had been wearing a black beanie. The police knew that David was known to wear a similar beanie. After all, given the many times they'd stopped him on the street to add to the dossier of his life, they pretty much knew all the clothes David was known to wear. Fully confident that David was not guilty of what he'd been accused of, we immediately drove him down to the station so we could put the matter behind us. Petrified beyond consoling, David was placed in a lineup, a motel maid said he was not the robber, and they let him go. This became what we now describe as the "beanie incident," and it went a long way toward reinforcing David's paranoia of the police.

If you have a child who is handicapped or has suffered a brain injury, you become hypersensitive to any indication that your child is not getting a fair shake in life. You acquire a specially tuned Geiger counter in your mind that amplifies potential scenarios of injustice. The fact that your child has already endured a senseless tragedy is reason enough to be concerned that other senseless things can and will happen. Sadly, what you eventually learn, especially as your child grows into adulthood, is not to put too much faith in people's ability to be compassionate and understanding. While you will find many decent people in the world who have your child's best interest in mind, you'll discover many more who are indifferent. Some can be downright abusive. You'll also have to learn to pick your battles to preserve your sanity and to keep the longevity of your family's well-being in mind.

All things considered, our family, which now included our new son-in-law, arrived at the consensus that it was time to move out of Utah. Once again, we loaded up the convoy, this time setting the heading "North to the Future."

CHAPTER 17

GUILT BY ASSOCIATION

Gena and I, along with David, headed due north out of Utah, eventually crossing the border into Canada via Montana. Dana and Stix diverted through Washington State and crossed north of Seattle. Border guards delayed them for a night, because Leeloo the python didn't have a pet passport. It could have been worse for the newlyweds. They could have brought their zoo full of reptiles and might have needed dozens of pet permits and passports. But prior to leaving Ivins, Stix sold every animal with the exception of his prized albino python, thus pocketing hundreds of greenbacks. His eighty-plus baby chameleons were fetching thirty bucks a tail.

In fact, we all sold everything that didn't have sentimental value. Using a commercial mover at this time averaged a dollar a pound to ship, so we eliminated everything that might cost us less to repurchase in Alaska. Selling one's junk, even at rock-bottom prices, is extremely cathartic. Everyone should try such an experience at least once in their lives, even if they're not moving. Call it a cleansing of the soul. Just get rid of all the crap and clutter, the mind-boggling surplus of stupid stuff you have accumulated throughout a lifetime of hoarding things, as well as the purging of bad thoughts and ruminations. Lighten your load. Eliminate materialism. Cut your toxic and cumbersome emotional ties. Maybe even get a new job or profession. Try changing your old life for the life you've always wanted as fast as you'd change from work clothes into sweats. This does the soul good.

We met up with Dana and Stix in Dawson Creek, Canada, and were together for the rest of the trip. Prior to leaving Utah, I'd bought a thirty-two-foot fifth-wheel trailer. The trailer provided plenty of space and beds for everyone to crash in. Dana had pictures of black bears and bison on her camera, which proved they'd seen more wildlife coming up through British Columbia than we did traveling through the interior. Stopping to soak in the clear pools of Liard Hot Springs in northern British Columbia was a treat. Liard consists of half a dozen natural pools, all with varying degrees of water temperature, tucked under the canopy of deciduous trees in a shallow valley. To get to the springs, you have to walk from a parking area over a wooden gangplank, which zigzags through marshland steaming with the pungent aroma of sulfur.

Traveling the Alaska Highway is one heck of a long road trip everyone should drive—once. With the exception of the few places to gas up, the vast majority of this concrete nature trail cuts through tundra that is as pristine now as it was hundreds of thousands of years ago. Think wild, think unspoiled, think prehistoric; think of isolation and what it means to feel insignificant. And then imagine not escaping

Picking Wings Off Butterflies

these thoughts for a few long weeks and the experience is summed up. Of course, one could make the trip in half a week at the speed of blur, but then they'd be better off flying. A year later, I actually did fly my way up in the cockpit of my Piper Arrow airplane while getting a bird's-eye view of the same length of highway, which also doubled as a convenient runway if I would have had engine trouble.

Our family convoy arrived in Soldotna in early May under a light drizzle and in the midst of the snow and ice breakup. We pulled into an RV park on the Crooked Creek adjacent to the Kasilof River. I freed my Chevy truck of the monkey on its back by unhitching the trailer. Stix and Dana moved into their own apartment less than a week after we arrived. David stayed with us for a few months, but we eventually got him his own place.

The ensuing months were marked by the Kenai and Kasilof Rivers' migration of kings, sockeyes, and silver salmon fish, along with the successive flow of incoming tourists. Summer sped by, as revealed by the blooming fireweed flowers and their display of seedpods, which turn in autumn into whispery wads of white like old men's beards. Late October turned cold with a vengeance. I winterized the trailer, and Gena and I stayed in a dinky blue cabin for a few months. In February, the house we had hired a contractor to build was completed, and we moved in just as the temperature was nipping at minus ten.

David got off to his new start like water seeking low ground. Back in St. George, there was only one official bar, appropriately named "The One and Only." But Kenai and Soldotna provided many more options for David to find companionship, which was often in bars where he knew people would accept him without prejudice.

David doesn't like the taste of beer, wine, or mixed

drinks. We joke with him about the faces of disgust he makes while drinking. What he likes on occasion is the buzz of alcohol that dulls the harsh realities of his world. Every day he wakes up is another day for him to realize that he is never going to fit into this world. He knows bars don't offer him the best of environments. Bars merely offer him a place to socialize. As his parents, Gena and I naturally tried to explain to him that the bar scene is not necessarily a safe or happy scene. While there are exceptions, bars are not the places where one creates lifetime friends and opportunities to better one's future. Not being one to listen to good advice, David inevitably was going to be in the wrong bar at the wrong place and time.

We learned of David's arrest like people often do when a friend or loved one has been arrested: by being on the receiving end of the only phone call they are entitled to make from jail, the call made infamous in so many true-crime dramas. Admittedly, it was a call I expected to receive at some point in my life—just not so soon. But I'd imagined such a scenario to occur at some point with David, not because David ever showed any signs of having a deviant criminal mind, but because of the track record he had in the past with the police and how people generally took advantage of him due to his handicaps.

Although the day we received the call was in July, one of the most temperate months of the year on the Kenai, I could not tell you whether the day was balmy, the wind brisk, the sky filled with whipped high-level clouds, or whether it was darkened by the brooding potentialities of a storm sweeping northward from Seward. I can only relate that driving out to my local county jail to visit my imprisoned son was an excursion of despair.

From the parking lot, Gena and I walked to the main

Picking Wings Off Butterflies

entrance and read the prohibitions on the posted sign. We patted ourselves down to make sure we didn't have any contraband. We peered up at the video camera eyeing us suspiciously and pressed the button. An unseen jailer buzzed us through the gate. We walked through another door and into a waiting room, where we sat fidgeting until another officer came out of another door and checked our driver's licenses. The officer then led us through another security door, where we sat and waited in front of a window covered with palm prints. I offered Gena the steel stool nearest the window, while I sat on a bench behind her and leaned against a cold cement wall. A black phone receiver hung to our left near the window. David was escorted in wearing a set of yellow jumpers and canvas slip-on shoes. The officer let David out of his handcuffs, and we talked.

Later I would have David write down his first impressions of what it's like going to the big house:

Jail detainment means being stuck in a room about the size of the TV room at my parents' house. Concrete floor, concrete bench, that's right I said bench. There's only one in there. Concrete walls, concrete ceiling, no windows, four Styrofoam mats, three blankets, a metal toilet with no privacy, and fifteen guys I've never seen in my life. And they must not believe in a heater in detainment, because it was freezing the whole time I was there.

So, nine hours later, I'm cold, I'm hungry, and still scared out of my mind. They take me into the strip room. Whatever you have been told about the strip room is pretty much what happens. To describe it thoroughly with one word would be to say that it is degrading. Finally, they get their act together and take me out of detainment into mod 4 where I would spend the next four days of my life on edge. I'm wondering what the people will be like in there, but who should I see upon entering the general population? My good friend Sam, another client from rehab.

At four in the morning a cop woke me up, took me out of my cell, and cuffed me. He lead me down the hallway into another room. He sat me in a chair and swabbed my mouth [DNA test]. Then he locked me back in my cell.

Well, the alarm goes off at 6:00 a.m. Breakfast is at 7:15 a.m. Why wake us up at 6:00 a.m. to do checks to make sure no one has escaped from the most highly guarded place I've seen in my life? While you trade breakfast items with other cellmates you realize that we don't get coffee upon arrival. Well, I'm a coffeeholic. So, I'm like, well that sucks. Turns out you don't get coffee until you earn the credits. But being that it was my second day there, I didn't have any credits earned. So, I traded my oatmeal to this biker looking dude named Bear for coffee.

Then the medication lady comes and gives us our meds [tuberculosis test and David's Prozac] and makes sure we take them and goes away. This is followed by the cop with a bucket full of shaving razors, totally generic, and waits by the doors until every prisoner returns their razor. Then it's game time. Well, not really. They had checkers and a few other games. But most of us go back to bed. I remember each cell had to be swept and mopped, toilets cleaned, beds made up every morning. Lunch was at 12:45 p.m. followed by lockdown. This means that the prisoners were locked in their cell for one hour. Then checks again, which I thought was pointless. You could be a genius and you'd never escape this place. There are cameras all over the place. Everything everyone does is on tape.

The games continue until 5:30 p.m. and it's dinner time followed by check again and game time. Then it's bedtime in which they do not shut your lights off. The beds are metal with a thin Styrofoam pad covered with a very thin blanket. Because the beds are metal, they pop really loud whenever you move, which doesn't allow for much sleep. This is followed by checks every thirty minutes of the night. And it goes on like this for four days.

Needless to say, I was on the brink of a nervous breakdown well before the fourth day there.

David spent the weekend after his arrest in jail. At his arraignment the following Monday, we were fortunate the judge set no bail. In lieu of bail, Gena and I agreed to watch David as third-party custodians. This meant David had to be visible or within earshot of us twenty-four hours a day, seven days a week, for an indefinite period of time. We greatly underestimated the emotional strain the conditions third-party release would have on our family. The alternative was worse, to let David remain in prison for months and months until his trial.

A few months prior to David's arrest, Gena and I had purchased two small music stores. We had previously operated the hospices together, but neither one of us had run a retail business. Additionally, we knew little about the music business. I played drums for a few bands in my younger years and was vaguely familiar with the instruments and equipment bands needed to play and record music. Gena plays flute and piano and knows quite a bit about orchestra instruments. So just like we did when we starting out building our hospices, we divvied up responsibilities and tasks as they presented themselves. At the time of David's arrest, the busy part of the retail season was bearing down on us. The previous owners of the music stores had agreed to work with us for a few months while we learned the business and longer if needed on a consulting basis. There were initial contracts that needed to be renegotiated to carry products for a dozen plus companies. There were orders that needed to be filled to increase stock for the upcoming school year and Christmas season. The music industry had changed astonishingly since I played back in the eighties, most notably in the area of electronics. Aside from the instruments associated with playing in a rock-and-roll band, there were now literally hundreds of electronic gizmos and gadgets we had to learn about in order to sell products. In our two stores alone, we had over three thousand unique products and dozens of kinds of instruments. Additionally, each instrument came in many different brands and models, and we needed to get up to speed quickly on everything we were selling. But there was much more to learn than what was in our mom-and-pop stores. We were also in the midst of planning a big grand opening with live music and free food. There were also employee concerns and many other details that had to be worked through. The workload was much more than we anticipated. Even so, those initial months were tremendously satisfying for me, because I really enjoyed the challenge of learning a new business, as well as helping local musicians and advocating for music in the community.

We started taking care of David as third-party custodians at the worst possible moment while in the process of learning and succeeding at our new business. Court stipulations demanded that David remain practically by our side. About the only thing we could do was sit David in the back office where we could watch him. If for some reason he wandered off and an officer dropped by, we could also be subject to criminal proceedings. The back room became a war zone where we were forced to endure David's incessant needs, deal with the legalities of his predicament, and then walk out into the showroom as though life was perfectly normal.

Picking Wings Off Butterflies

When the workday ended, like normal folks we had errands to run and shopping to do. Sometimes we went out to eat. But due to the stipulations of David's third-party release, we had to make sure that we didn't take David into a store or a restaurant that served alcohol. This limited our restaurant choices to a few local fast-food restaurants. If we went grocery shopping, one of us had to wait in the car with David, since there was a section for alcohol in both of the local grocery stores. One of our close friends commented to us that we were probably the best third-party participants the state had ever seen. I'm not sure about this, but we had learned—much like David learned—to expect the worst when he's involved. If David could be snatched away from us by a servant of the law, because he accidentally walked through the liquor aisle on his way to the bathroom, then he probably would be.

Eight months after his arrest, I reached a level of despondency I never thought I could exceed, only to be forced to push far beyond this threshold into dimensions of despair I never thought possible.

CHAPTER 18

OUR NATIONAL SHAME

*W*hen I began helping David tell his story, I hoped that he and I would be able to write our journey together in a way that inspired others. These would be parents with handicapped children, families who have raised children with severe head injuries, medical and other professionals needing insight into the complexities of traumatic brain injuries, teachers who might be struggling with how to better educate and integrate the "intellectually challenged" into the world, and anyone else who might gain inspiration from his story. Given his arrest, this objective now seems more daunting than ever.

Regarding the circumstances surrounding David's arrest, I believe he was singled out because of his head injuries. In other words, he was judged to be a person who lacked certain mental capabilities, and this resulted in a bias that caused the individuals responsible for his

Picking Wings Off Butterflies

incarceration to believe he had impure motives for his actions. This is the only reason I can come up with, because he was punished for doing something that many people have done and continue to do all around the world every single day, but because these individuals are not perceived to be intellectually handicapped, they will never be punished for the same kind of infraction. Unfortunately, for legal reasons, I'm not at liberty to elaborate, except to state what's in the public record. He was babysitting for his friend and arrested for disciplining her children by spanking them. The public record of his case is readily accessible to anyone who desires to investigate further, so I have no reason to deny its contents. Quite the contrary, what David was accused of doing and charged with should concern any parent or guardian. But as most people would readily acknowledge, what really happens with any legal case is always heavily supported by the backstory; the off-the-record kind of stuff. So, even if I were to spend the next couple of chapters accurately conveying precisely what transpired, my attempt would likely prove futile. Additionally, I would run the risk of sounding accusatorial and revengeful to others involved with his case, which I have no desire to do. Granted, these details might make for salacious prime-time fodder (and perhaps give this book more mass appeal), but that was never the intent David and I set out with, and this book was never meant to be a true-crime drama.

These things having necessarily been said, and with your permission, I will for the next few pages suspend my politically correct tone and sharpen the fangs of my prose, because there is a permissible way in which I can defend David's honor, and it is by offering a few astute observations regarding the criminal justice system. I offer these observations primarily to provide insight into the judicial processes for the general public, and as a tale of caution for individuals with traumatic brain injuries or those with other special needs who may also find themselves victimized by the system some day.

At this point I feel that you should have a clear understanding of the kind of person David is despite his head injuries. Overall, he's a kind and thoughtful person who would do anything to help a friend, and he possesses a high degree of compassion that prevents him from knowingly and willfully harming another person. Indeed, he has never physically harmed anyone. As I've revealed, he can lack foresight and judgment at times, and he did a few stupid things while negotiating adolescence—but didn't we all? My point is that David doesn't possess a criminal mind. I define a criminal mind as a brain controlled by an incessant train of thoughts engaged in planning and carrying out actions with the intent to physically or emotionally hurt people. And David's mind, albeit rattled a bit due to his accident, is not preoccupied with these kinds of thoughts. Like the average normal person, he does and says stupid things sometimes, but he is not a deviant or diabolical person by any definition of these terms. I realize I'm entrusting you to believe my characterization of David without filling in much of the details regarding his legal battle, but as I said above, the record of what transpired in his case is readily available, and his story was never meant to be prime-time fodder.

What will not be most obvious to many, however, is how a head injury or a specific intellectual or physical handicap influences a person's behavior. Even less clear—and this is the crux of the matter—is how to appropriately punish individuals who may from time to time break a law or, in David's case, simply cross a socially unacceptable line. Suffice it to say, our understanding of how to compassionately

Picking Wings Off Butterflies

help and rehabilitate individuals with special needs is infantile, and the current solutions to which we treat these individuals—often by locking them up—is willfully crude if not medieval.

If you are still following my trail of logic, consider this: If you ask a random sampling of people with emotional and intellectual handicaps if people treat them with the equality and respect afforded to otherwise normal people, they would indicate with a resounding NO! In all likelihood, these individuals are being ostracized due to their handicaps (by family, friends, and the general public), and in many cases they are even being harassed by those who feel the need to exercise power over their lives. Which begs the question, Is it possible that many intellectually handicapped individuals are being unjustly targeted, criminally prosecuted, and subsequently incarcerated for crimes that the average person would never be punished for? YES! Of course they are, as any cursory examination of the system would reveal. Which brings me back full circle in my attempt to offer a partial explanation as to why David became an easy scapegoat and target for our judicial system.

The thing is, David is profoundly fearful of the police. David would admit to just about anything, because he wholeheartedly believes that the police can and will use force to get people to confess anything, even if it's something they did not do. David's objective was, and always has been, self-preservation, but also to avoid physical pain. His anxieties are in part caused by his previous experiences with the profiling done by law enforcement officers toward him and are further enhanced due to the handicaps in his thought processes caused as a result of his head injuries. Frankly, David is not capable of fully understanding his rights, and he lacks the ability to discern how to truthfully and yet, objectively, answer questions from law enforcement. Consequently, when read his Miranda rights at the time of his arrest, David did not take advantage of his *right to remain silent*, and what he did say was definitely *used against* him. Had David waited until he had legal representation, he would have had the necessary information and legal guidance to truthfully express himself in a manner that I believe would not have led to his incarceration.

In other words, a person with a head injury who has a history of being harassed by the police, and who believes their questioner can physically assault them, is no match for a professional in a position of power who has been trained to psychologically coax answers even out of rational and intelligent people. Which is why, in cases involving individuals with head injuries, certain accommodations should be considered. Simply put, laws should be established for individuals with established head injuries that would ensure these individuals always have legal representation present when they are questioned by the police, because these individuals are likely to inadvertently incriminate themselves (or other innocents) even when they're not guilty of committing a crime.

Now, after having been exposed to the American judicial system through David's case, I must admit that my long-standing opinions regarding its role in our culture have been embarrassingly naive. I've now been enlightened, so to speak, and the following criticisms will no doubt seem over the top for those who remain blissfully unaware and uninitiated. But trust me on this, if you ever step foot in a courthouse and have to experience the judicial process from start to finish—if you have any ethical sense of what is right and wrong—you will come to recognize how dysfunctional the American justice system really is. And I'd venture to

Picking Wings Off Butterflies

say that you will come to this realization even if the system works entirely in your favor and you win the outcome you sought. Because even if you do win, you'll be breathing a sigh of relief when your case is finally over and you realize that with all the shenanigans that took place, you probably won just out of sheer luck.

So, in brief, my forthright indictment on the system is thus:

The American prison system, once primarily run by government agencies to rehabilitate individuals, has for many years offered a lucrative investment option for individuals and businesses wanting a slice of this American pie for their investment portfolios. Currently, at the present rate at which our government is creating and enforcing laws, the industry can't throw up cement fortifications fast enough to meet the supply and demand for what can only be described as human product. It no longer represents what it was intended to represent: an institution created to rehabilitate individuals back into society or to compassionately house those deemed too dangerous for this possibility. Rather, it has become yet another avenue to embellish upon the inherent greed of capitalism—and worse—a place where society dumps its undesirables. The statistical data regarding the percentages of citizens we cast into our dungeons is becoming our national shame, surpassing even those countries that we have long criticized for human rights abuses. What's common knowledge? That the land of the free throws more of its people in prison than any other country in the world! Period.

No doubt, many who work within the judicial system can relate to my frank commentary. The system employs a vast army of people such as court clerks, janitors, correctional officers, peace officers, professional witnesses, lawyers, judges, and so, so many others. At its philosophical core, the system is an organization built for the people and by the people, and there are many decent, hardworking individuals who work in the system and who are genuinely concerned with the welfare of those who are being punished and rehabilitated. Overall, I believe the individuals who find employment within the system have a genuine desire to help the incarcerated, as well as to contribute positively to the betterment of society. But I have no doubt that they also recognize the polarity that exists between the moral and ethical foundation to which the system purports to represent and what they actually see taking place within every stage of the judicial process from a person's arrest, to trial, to incarceration. I'm certain that this dichotomy causes many of them great consternation, and they wish the system could be better.

If I seem flippant, it's for good reason. Because for twenty-six years, Gena and I have nurtured and protected our beloved son with two noble goals in mind: to help him be a responsible adult and to help him find his place in this world. (And we did this not only for personal reasons but also for the benefit of our society.) We have weathered the worst that life has thrown his way. We have fought teachers and school administrators to get him an education, written letters to state workers to push for job and educational training, counseled with dozens of medical professionals to ensure that David was psychologically and emotionally healthy, and raised him to be a decent and kind person with strong moral values. David could barely get a job with a head injury—but at least it was a possibility. Where once David had a chance to get off state and federal welfare programs, his legal record will now likely keep him unemployable and living off taxpayers indefinitely. Twenty-six years down the drain in literally the blink of an eye—and for naught—and

Picking Wings Off Butterflies

why? Why is it that we tolerate a judicial system that ruins the lives of so many of our citizens while simultaneously leading to the dilapidation of our society?

A peculiar phenomenon happens to honest, patriotic, and hardworking people when confronted with injustice. Upstanding citizens begin to wonder what the hell is happening to the country they love. What they experience is an erosion of trust in their government and elected officials, which has both a trickle-up and a trickle-down effect. Initially, the reality sets in that one does not have the particular freedoms and rights they naively assumed, and they begin to question the intrusion of big government in their lives. With this there comes distrust toward state and city representatives, judges, and lawyers, and this distrust eventually trickles down to being wary of the role of local law enforcement. Simultaneously, one begins to recognize that their representatives in Washington also do not have the best interest of the people in mind. Like a sleeping giant, good citizens confronted with injustice are forced to wise up one day and recognize that they have been too complacent for far too long. They then become what I call reluctantly good citizens.

What's a reluctantly good citizen (RGC)? Essentially, an RGC is an otherwise good and productive citizen who realizes that the system they have supported is corrupt and likely broken beyond repair. And also, that many who hold positions of power have lost their moral compass. If the RGC is not careful, he or she will be tempted to lose his or her own ethical way. After all, if the representatives of the people in our great land can no longer be trusted to do the right thing, then how can they expect the average citizen to do the right thing? However, the most significant word represented by the acronym RGC is *reluctant*. For the good citizen—the one who truly cares—losing faith in his country or his fellow citizens is not an option. One thing is certain: the only thing any RGC can do is to pick up the whistle and blow, to fight for equality and justice, and to try and influence the right kind of people in the right places to forge positive change.

And yet, I have another observation to point out, one that appeals to the heart and our sense of compassion. In all my visits to my local courthouse, there seems to be an extraordinary percentage of the poor, the powerless, the downtrodden—and yes, the handicapped—who are being punished for breaking the laws. As the accused, they shuffle into the courtroom wearing different-colored jumpsuits designating the severity of the crimes they've been charged with. The felons are wearing yellow jumpers, and the misdemeanors are sporting blue jumpers. Every one of the "innocents until proven guilty" is bound with handcuffs and ankle chains, and then linked together with a rung of additional chains like in a cheap B-rated horror flick. There are folks being accused of crimes who have mental and physical handicaps like David. There are individuals in for drug abuse. There are people in for drinking too much alcohol and smoking a weed. Others are guilty of getting into bar fights, spouses in for domestic spats, and others in for petty theft. I know that from time to time those who hold positions of prestige in the community have broken the law, but I have yet to see one such accused in the courtroom even for the infractions I just mentioned. I also recognize that from time to time there are individuals who have been accused of serious crimes, and the severity of their crimes warrants the security measures imposed upon them. But I'm truly horrified by the spectacle of seeing the handicapped, poor, emotionally and intellectually challenged, and just the average down-on-their-luck citizens shuffling into the courtroom with security measures better suited for a serial killer, bearing morbid expressions of embarrassment and self-loathing.

I mean no disrespect—just brutal honesty. At each hearing, Gena and I sat in the spectators' arena, as do the other parents, relatives, and friends of the accused. We are protected and isolated behind a waist-high wall and sit on cushioned seats. There is pomp and protocol in the proceedings that follow. The state's representatives walk in prepared for battle with either a mountain of files tucked under their arms or, as I've seen on a number of occasions, wheeling in boxes of paperwork on a dolly. There is commitment in the faces of the defending lawyers who seem genuinely concerned for their client's well-being. They also appear overworked and overwhelmed by the magnitude of their caseloads. The court guards look bored, but they are courteous. The judge of the day is always matter-of-fact, knowledgeable, and seems ready to consider the interests of all parties. The judge is also quick to defend her honor when she feels it has been compromised or not adequately acknowledged through the usage of proper court etiquette. (I once had the opportunity to say a few words at the podium on David's behalf and was chastised for not removing my hat.) The court reporter moves through her business with typographical precision without saying a word. The accused unconsciously rattle their chains and look rightfully tormented. The atmosphere is pungent with severity. Every motion and procedure moves along with liturgical precision in which the stakes for the accused have the potential to be life-changing.

I made unconventional connections as I sat there watching my brain-injured son being prosecuted while infractions of monumental immorality went unchecked beyond the courthouse walls:

I thought of the billions of dollars in war profiteering being made in Iraq, Afghanistan, and other locales at the expense of human lives.

I thought of the unethical infractions of corporate CEOs who will ruin the lives of thousands of people today through mismanagement and walk away with a king's ransom for a job well done.

I thought of the actions of the bankers, traders, and executives of Wall Street, which, during the time David was being prosecuted, were carrying on practices that would later render millions of American citizens jobless and countless families with children homeless, and the way they skirted justice by never even getting a slap on the wrist.

I thought of individuals working for medical insurance companies that will deny medical coverage to their paying customers and effectively sentence many fellow citizens to death.

I thought of the rich and powerful who have the necessary funds and influence to buy their own brand of justice.

I thought of famous celebrities who committed crimes far worse than the infractions David was accused of committing and who were granted leniency because they entertained us.

Finally, I reflected on the millions of dollars being pocketed through the lucrative business of imprisoning American citizens, and the role of our elected officials in creating and condoning laws that lead to the incarceration of our most helpless and needy citizens.

And there my son sits, the left side of his face still drooping in a permanent, delicate frown.

Picking Wings Off Butterflies

Yet, in my mind I have always visualized David as an emerging butterfly; filled with so much beauty and potential and ever ready to take flight into a promising life of his choosing. But at seemingly every milestone in his life events have transpired to prevent his metamorphosis.

He never hurt anyone and this would include the children he was babysitting. Indeed, the prosecuting attorney confessed at a pretrial hearing that never at any point were there any observations of injuries or bruising on the children, and that created a very huge issue as far as the state was concerned as to reasonable doubt. He also stated he had reservations that David would be convicted of any of the charges brought against him had the case gone to trial. After hearing this, I wanted to cry foul, but after glancing around the courtroom I could find no referee. And yet despite the state's confession, it still saw fit to pick the wings off my remarkable butterfly and ensure that he never be given the opportunity to fly.

Now, I do not necessarily condone the practice of spanking, but it is a common form of discipline and one likely used by others who sat in the courtroom the day in which *only* my son was sent to jail for it. Nor do I condone the use illegal drugs, or harming one's spouse, or stealing. However, what is disturbing is the priority and ease to which the American justice system will imprison individuals with traumatic brain injuries like David, (as well as others who possess similar mental, emotional, and physical challenges) while oftentimes turning a blind judicial eye to the kinds of white-collar crimes I alluded to above.

CHAPTER 19

LETTERS FROM JAIL

    *P*risoners brandishing handcrafted weapons, riots in the courtyard, gangs vying for territory and respect, trading food for favors, terror in the showers—I tried to visualize what David must have been feeling as he mentally prepared to be rehabilitated for his crimes. Not having been to jail, I only knew what I'd witnessed on television and heard by way of street talk. Surely the movies and documentaries described jail as more bleak than it really was? But for David, television *is* reality. These two channels of life are interchangeable. What would David do when one of the prisoners on his block took the fish sticks off his aluminum lunch tray or reached for his cookie? How would David handle it if he was confronted in the shower to perform sex acts? What kinds of problems would David run into with his cell mate? Would David join a gang for protection? Would he become somebody's bitch or a prison guard's snitch?

    David must have been going through hell. Never quick

on his feet, he moved about the house with the pace of a sloth. Always easily distracted, he has never been able to sit still and focus on one thing for more than a few minutes at a time. Usually he's jumping between reading, playing video games, or watching movies. Not so these days as his mindset had radically changed. Instead, he sat for long periods of time, pensively staring into space, contemplating every jailhouse scene he'd ever witnessed on television, as though he was working out the details in his head of what he was going to do when each challenge presented itself.

Alas, the day arrived for David's final court appearance; the day he would be sentenced and taken back into custody to serve his time. Gena, Dana, and I were all present. We knew David was going away, but there would be no need to pack his suitcase. We needed only to gather his medication together: Ambien for sleep, Prozac for anxiety, and the desmopressin nasal spray for his diabetes insipidus. Gena put his meds in a Ziploc bag and told David to keep the bag in the pocket of his sweatshirt until he checked into jail. We all gave David a big hug before he had to join his lawyer on the other side of the wall opposite the spectators. David's lawyer informed the court that David was remanding himself into custody. Other than his family members, no one in the court had any emotional reaction to the fact that David was going to jail. This was routine. He was sentenced to six months in prison and five years of probation. It could have been far worse. David could been sentenced to several years, but he took the plea deal (notorious for securing confessions of guilt) offered by the state.

Contrary to what he'd been told to do, David whipped out his baggie full of drugs. The judge wagged her head, and there was a noticeable hush. Legal drugs or not, drugs and courtrooms do not mix. I was thinking, *They don't know what they've got themselves into. They* being those who have no clue what it's going to be like taking care of a person with a brain injury. They thought they'd be rehabilitating a hardened criminal. What they'd really be doing was something far less noble. I was sure that by the end of the first week, most of the corrections officers would be wondering why David ever set foot on their turf in the first place.

I felt like a traitor. What kind of father willingly leads his son to jail when he's certain his son doesn't deserve to be there? Why didn't I do more? We paid for a lawyer, but should I have hired a high-powered defense team? Unfortunately, I didn't have deep enough pockets to buy a team of lawyers to prove his innocence. Powerless, that's what I felt—powerless.

A few days later, we visited David at his new residence. As we'd hoped, David was placed in a general holding facility at the county jail, as opposed to being sent hours away or even relocated to a federal prison in the lower forty-eight states. After getting "clicked" through the main gate, Gena and I entered another door leading into the small waiting area with stained carpet. There was a sign on the wall with a phone number offering visitors a financial reward to tattle on other citizens who they thought might be violating the law—in effect, to help fill the cages with more people. Anonymity was promised. I wondered how people could remain anonymous and still collect their reward.

An officer entered the room about five minutes prior to the top of the visiting hour through another door. He recorded our names and addresses, gave us a quick sweep with his weapon-detecting wand, and led us into a visiting chamber with three stalls. David shuffled in a few minutes later. He took a seat on the other side of the glass, and we communicated through handheld receivers.

Picking Wings Off Butterflies

What do you say to your beloved child when you first visit him in jail? What can you say when you know your conversation is being recorded?

Why, Dave, you're looking particularly cheerful this morning! Love the outfit. You look great in yellow. Those shoes look comfortable but a little big. You're shivering. Don't they issue you jackets in here? What's that? They don't issue warm clothes, but you can buy sweat suits in the jail store? You're kidding, right? Who's the owner of the store? I wonder what his profit margin is with such a captive clientele. Don't worry, we'll give you money to buy clothes to stay warm. (Actually, I just asked him how he was doing.)

But I could see he was looking pretty good, despite the fact that he was freezing and only into the first week of what would be months of incarceration. In fact, he was surprisingly at peace considering his circumstances. I'd been worried he was going to be so depressed that they might have to put him on a suicide watch. But I was right proud of the lad. I suppose, had he actually been guilty of committing a real crime worthy of his punishment, I might have been embarrassed he was my son. The fact that he so bravely stood up to injustice filled me full of pride.

Ironically, it was David who was concerned about what his mother and father were going through, which further impressed me.

He said, "I'm fine. It's okay. You don't have to worry about me. I've got friends, and a couple of guys have got my back." Once again, David's skill in winning friends was paying off.

After this first visit, we settled into a routine of visiting him once a week. Dana and Stix tried to visit him every Sunday. An added advantage was that David could call us anytime, so we usually spoke with him at least once a day when he called the music store. David also wrote letters, which let us know what was going through his mind while he did his time.

> *June 14*
>
> *Dear mom, dad, or whoever else might be listening. How is it going? I am doing fine. I've learned to take life one day at a time and not to dwell on what the future holds, because it's overriding my brain to the point of anxiety.*
>
> *Now for some sarcasm. My life on a normal day in here. It's 5:30 a.m. I know this because ever since coming here I'm always up thirty minutes before the breakfast bell at six. Yeah, up but not out of bed. Depending on who checks into Comfort Inn number 416, I may or may not have a celly or another inmate living with me. Today, no celly. Soon enough six o'clock comes as does the sun in my room, which shines 24/7. [David referred to the lights in his cell block that were always on as "the sun."]*
>
> *Now for the surprise breakfast, which believe it or not is edible. Yummy. It's an egg muffin sandwich. Next I stroll back to my cell to make sure it's clean for inspection time for Mr. Clean. Medication count at 7:00 a.m., and every Monday, Wednesday, Friday laundry at 8:00 a.m. After that it's game time, same games every day, but different conversation topics. If I get bored I can always go back to bed, which usually happens anyhow. Lunch rolls in at 11:00 a.m. We eat and have lockdown until 12:30 p.m., and then the afternoons play out pretty much like the morning until dinner at 4:00 p.m., and*

then games again until lockdown for the night at 11:00 p.m.

I think about you guys all the time and somehow I get by. Ten more weeks of this bullshit and it will be time to start my new life on probation, but out of trouble. There will not be a repeat of the previous lifestyles I can guarantee that. I am all for becoming a better person. Now one of the things that has helped considerably is my relationship with God, which is something I plan to continue when I get out, though there will be many obstacles in my way I will survive to be a better person.

Love David

P.S. Enclosed are some abstract drawings. Thanks dad for your support in my life, and all the little tips you gave me on making my art stand out.

On the road to becoming a better person, David got into a little trouble while taking some food a fellow inmate had offered him. David said that one evening he walked upstairs to a friend's cell. Jimmy was lying on his bunk reading a book, and David struck up a conversation with him while standing just outside his door. Jailhouse rules stipulated that prisoners were not allowed to step foot in each other's cells, but prisoners could chat with each other through open doors.

David spotted a box of breakfast bars on Jimmy's shelf. "Can I have one of those?" he asked.

"Yeah, but you'll have to grab it yourself if you want it."

David dashed into Jimmy's cell, grabbed a bar, and ran back out. A corrections officer sitting in a nearby monitoring room saw David running out of Jimmy's cell. "Stahlecker. LOCK DOWN!" he yelled.

David shuffled back to his cell and had three hours of time-out until the officer let him out later that night. David might have been alone that evening, but he didn't go hungry!

July 4

Dear mom, thank you for your letter. I appreciate the support I've been getting from everyone back home. I really miss it (being there), but for now I have to deal with the fact that this is my home for the time being. Eight more weeks of this and I'll be home, back where I belong.

Do me a favor. Check the pet shops for a large macaw. Any color is OK, but I prefer red, green, or white, and a young one. I think it will be good company for me to have as a pet. I watched a little of the movie "Over the Hedge." From what I remember I liked the movie.

I hope I can work when I get out. I want to be a normal boy.

My finding God, that's a big deal for me. I've always known it would be since I was a little kid. Although I never talked about it, it was always a big thing on my mind. In a way I always had delayed that relationship simply because I knew it would mean I would have to—to some extent—give up on all the things I had a lust for. Simply put, I would have to let God reprogram me, and because of the interests I had in earthly or materialistic possessions and objects. But I finally came to the point in my life recently where I realized that me working through life by myself is setting me up to fail. So I began to pray and give up my lust of the mind, and felt the presence of God come to me and it did. And ever since then I commit myself to doing the best I can for myself.

I'm learning to strive for excellence daily and to think before every action and word. The top two things on my to-do list at present, mainly because this is not an experience I want to go through again (jail), it's one of those been there, done that things. So away with that past life shit and onward with the new and improved me. While I'm writing this I'll also be sending some more artwork. It is now past midnight and I need to sleep to be up for breakfast at six, so tootles.

Love David

The building in which David stayed had a common area where the prisoners could talk, read, play games, and watch television. One day the other prisoners let David watch a movie of his choice. He picked the Disney classic *Finding Nemo*. I would have picked *Con Air* starring Nicolas Cage. I would have picked practically any other movie to show what a tough guy I was. But my son, the convict, the threat to society, the citizen so in need of being rehabilitated, picks *Finding Nemo*.

July 19

Dear family. Five more weeks until freedom. Enclosed is a pic of the memorial tattoo I drew up to cover the homemade one on my left arm under Ozzy, but I'm still thinking of covering the Ozzy up too. It says my nickname Skootman and M. Bay BF4L. And actually, this one will cover the Ozzy. He's just not my hero anymore. [The memorial tattoo would be in memory of his friend Martin, who passed away in high school.]

Anyhow, the spelling to "M. Bay" is done in an abstract graffiti style of lettering. The "M" is done with the "B" merging into it. The "a" is drawn into the gap of the "m" lower cased and the "4" of the BF4U spelling is on top of the "k" in "Skootman." This tattoo I drew up will be the last one that I ever get.

Love David

July 26

Dear mom, dad, and the rest of the gang. Countdown, 4 more weeks to go. Thank you mom for your letter stating that I finally am a normal man. Geez. It took me forever to get that title, but I am proud to be included with the rest of them (normal men). I am even more proud of the level of maturity I find myself endowed with nowadays.

I can finally say I feel like a true adult with all the time I've had. The last three months I was able to sort out my mind and get rid of a few of the ideas I was supporting in the last year. Here's a small list: I am not skitzo. I am not dumb. I have smarts. I am not helpless. All hope is not lost. God is a must have for me in my life. The relationship I have with him makes for a very happy David. I know that deep down I am a quiet person, and not the lunatic I've played for so long. My OCD is a crock. I've mastered the art of controlling my outbursts, or the so called Tourette Syndrome. Yes we don't play like that anymore.

Love David

P.S. I redrew the tattoo and I'm sending you the picture. You can toss the other one.

Dana wanted to pick David up on the day he was finally set free. Although it was going to be at seven in the morning, she insisted. When Dana gets it in her head to do something, by golly, she's going to do it! She had plans after picking up David to take him to a breakfast buffet, then shopping, and then later to a Chinese buffet before finally letting Gena and me—his own parents, for crying out loud—see our son. We didn't even bother to challenge what she was planning for David, because she would not let us do what we wanted anyway.

So, she called us from the parking lot outside the main gate. "Mom," she said, "he's out—finally. And you're not going to believe this. They let him out without his shoes! He came out of the gate with just his socks on."

Indeed, the officers let him leave without shoes. He went in with shoes, but he came out with only socks. Of course, there's a perfectly good explanation for this slip-up, the story of which begins a few months back.

Gena and I had given David money to buy shoes at the jail commissary. He'd been sporting the jailhouse loafers since he arrived, but there were shoes at the commissary that the prisoners could purchase. David bought a pair from the store and, being the generous person that he is, he gave his prison shoes away to another prisoner who needed them.

Big mistake! Jailhouse rules specifically prohibited giving articles of clothing to other prisoners without prior approval. David would have known this had he read the rulebook he'd been given, but the thought never "occurred" to him how important this might be. David's breaking of the rules necessitated a full-blown investigation of said infraction. After being questioned, David was informed that in the near future he would be punished by being "thrown in the hole." This jailhouse expression meant David would get one week of isolation.

David never did get solitary confinement, because he was let out before he could be thrown in the hole. In retrospect, I believe the jailers were being nice to David. It's likely that they—much like everyone else learns after spending any time with David—concluded that he was not a threat. To my knowledge, David only got into trouble twice in jail: once for giving his shoes away to a needy prisoner, the other time for making a mad dash for the breakfast bar. The other prisoners may have thought David was a Goody Two-shoes. The jailers had to hold David to the same accountability as they did all the other prisoners, so I believe they delayed in seeing to his punishment. In effect, doing him a favor.

Even a dyslexic poet could appreciate the irony, that when David walked across the cold, pebbled parking lot in his socks to Dana's truck, he lacked not only the shoes he went into jail with but also the pair he bought from the commissary. His jailers told him they had misplaced his shoes and were looking for them while David was signing the paperwork needed for his release. When David finished his paperwork, they had not found his shoes yet, and David refused to wait any longer to get the hell out of jail. After leaving the compound, Dana ran him over to her apartment, where he grabbed a pair of Stix's size twelve boots before

Picking Wings Off Butterflies

heading out to the department store to buy him yet another pair of shoes.

When Dana finally got David over to our music store, I wrapped my arms around him. It was fantastic to have him with us again! The ordeal was over, but his new life as a convicted felon was just beginning.

David in Ivins, Utah, 2004

David's 25th birthday, Kasilof, Alaska, 2008

*The author and his wife Gena,
Bodega Bay, California, 2016*

Stix and Dana Jenkins in Palmer, Alaska, 2007

AFTERWORD

ONE YEAR LATER

David is still on probation, and this requires monthly visits with his probation officer. Knowing David, I'm not surprised probation has gone remarkably well. His life, of course, will never be the same. To name a few notable changes: While on probation, he won't be able to participate in our great democracy by voting. From now on, he'll have a difficult time obtaining decent housing due to discriminatory practices often used against felons. And he'll always have to check the box indicating he's a felon on employment applications, thus decreasing the likelihood of obtaining any form of employment and increasing the odds he'll survive on taxpayers' dollars for the rest of his life.

As for myself, I've continued to adopt less naive and more realistic viewpoints regarding my culture. More importantly, I've acquired the courage to at least speak my mind when I know these viewpoints can generate good discussion on important matters that lead to positive social changes. I think, for example, of the phrase "with liberty and justice for all." This phrase concludes the US Pledge of Allegiance written in 1892 by Francis Bellamy and is a truism that's taken on a new meaning for me. If your home has ever been robbed, you know that you lose more than a few *things* that the thief steals. You lose your sense of security and freedom. As an American citizen, I'm extremely grateful to live in a land that keeps me reasonably safe and my possessions secure. I also maintain a high level of respect for the individuals who wear uniforms and sacrifice their time (and often their lives) so I can enjoy these privileges. I'm also thankful to be free: free to think as I choose, free to believe as I choose, free to speak as I choose, and free of unwarranted governmental intrusions. These are indeed a lot of freedoms. But I now know that freedom and security are rapidly dissipating ideals. Injustice is hard enough to swallow when I (we) think of all the individuals who are not being treated with equal respect and dignity. But having the full power of the state bear down on your handicapped child causes you to be legitimately concerned about the lack of mercy and compassion meted out to the less fortunate within the American justice system.

I have effectively become the reluctantly good citizen. Which is to say, I understand how to treat people with dignity and respect. I believe most of my fellow citizens understand why cherishing these ideals is the only way to prevent our civilization from crumbling. The trouble is, these ideals are no longer being used as guiding principles in the political processes of our great land. The evidence for legislated favoritism is clearly seen in the growing divide between the rich and the poor, and the manner in which the wealthy and powerful are treated compared to the poor and defenseless. I believe that as a society we are approaching a threshold, a tipping point in which the challenge is thus: How do good, honest, and hardworking citizens do the right

Picking Wings Off Butterflies

thing when they can no longer trust their leaders to do the right thing? The most obvious answer is to continue doing the right thing, to continue being a good person and a good citizen. I offer yet another suggestion: People need to do what they can to fight for the values that made America great—namely, equality, freedom, and justice. My sincere hope is that David's life, as told through my eyes as his father, can contribute positively to this endeavor.

Yet, despite all that I have revealed about David in this book, I truly am proud of how far he has come and the person he has become. If fulfillment in life is measured by our individual journeys—meaning how we get from where we are to where we want to be—then David has overcome more trials and tribulations than most individuals. At the time of his accident, David lost more than his ability to eat, talk, and walk. He lost a considerable amount of his personality. He also lost points off his IQ, as well as bits and pieces of his emotional intelligence. What he has won back, however, are traits that really matter the most in life as far as I'm concerned. These traits are empathy and compassion. Many consider these qualities as weaknesses, but in actuality, these virtues are difficult to emulate. To be selfish to the point that one lacks the capacity to consider the needs of others is a primitive way of thinking. To have empathy and compassion, however, requires freeing oneself of one's own egocentric fixations. This requires far more effort and higher levels of thinking to accomplish.

As to the future, who knows? Surely things can't get any worse than they already have? This is what I keep asking myself. I buy into this wish through my tentative belief in karma but also because of my appreciation for statistics. David and I are far from being exemplary people. My family is far from representing the idyllic American clan. We're good people, though, who have lived honest, hardworking lives. Were I a betting man, I'd say the stats are looking increasingly better. We've also stacked plenty of karma chips in our favor. But honestly, I'm too practical these days to even speculate. For you see, roughly half the world lives on less than $2.50 a day. So, in rare moments, when I'm foolish enough to reminisce about how tough life has been for David and our family, I'm mindful of the billions of people in the world who have far less and endure so much more.

Will life get better for David? This is my real concern, and I pose a similar question for you. If you are suffering due to an illness or accident (or know someone who is), will life ever get better for you (or them)?

Naturally, I cannot know the answer to this question. I can only leave you with parting advice. The most positive mental attitude any individual with a TBI can have is hope. This also holds true for any person suffering from debilitating mental and physical conditions. The kind of hope I'm referring to is not wishful thinking. Nor does it represent an ethereal belief that promises to give a person capabilities he or she might not otherwise possess. Hope is best described as a *motivational energy* that materializes within the mind when a person visualizes a goal he or she wants to achieve. And I do mean materialize, because that motivational energy causes actual chemical and biological processes to occur in the brain that can help to reestablish or reroute lost connections, which are the cause of so many mental and physical impairments following a debilitating injury. This is a power you already possess, and it's an energy anyone can harness to propel the healing process that leads to a more fulfilled life.

TEN YEARS LATER, MAY 2017

Roughly a decade has passed since David's arrest. For reasons that I cannot fully understand it took me ten years to write and edit this book for publication. If I were to guess at the most obvious reason, it would be that I thought this book needed a longer incubation time to reflect on the events I wanted to cover, which bridged the gap from David's accident to his reaching adulthood. During this time, a lot has happened in David's life, in much the same way that time brings changes to all of our lives. The difference is, with David, the lows seem more dire and the highs more extreme, and the everyday occurrences still have me wagging my head and chuckling at how beautiful and bizarre life can be.

That said, I would like to conclude with this final reason for celebration:

In May of 2017, Gena and I boarded a plane heading towards Alaska to witness an event that signified one of the proudest moments of our lives: we watched David graduate from college! Through four long years he had been pushing well beyond his imagined limitations and earned an associate degree in Christian Ministry. It was a stunning accomplishment given his ongoing challenges. But I knew all along David was capable of such an achievement, because I have believed in him all my life. Watching him don his cap and gown and walk (still on his tip toes) into a new future was a wonderful sight that brought tears to Gena's eyes. This achievement should have an enormous impact on his self-esteem. I'm also hoping it will help him realize that he doesn't need to feel like a victim anymore, or that life has conspired against him, but that he can be a source of inspiration in the lives of other individuals. And although we once vowed to never, ever, under any circumstances, buy him another form of electronics . . . we bought him the bestest graduation gift of his choosing—a new gaming console!

Made in United States
North Haven, CT
03 September 2022